AMERICAN INDIAN
SECRETS OF
CRYSTAL HEALING

AMERICAN INDIAN SECRETS OF CRYSTAL HEALING

LUC BOURGAULT

BLUE EAGLE

quantum

LONDON • NEW YORK • TORONTO • SYDNEY

quantum

An imprint of W. Foulsham & Co. Ltd.
The Publishing House, Bennetts Close,
Cippenham, Berkshire, SL1 5AP, England

ISBN 0-572-02263-8

Printed in Great Britain by Creative Print & Design Wales, Ebbw Vale

ACKNOWLEDGEMENTS

I first want to thank the two people who helped me to understand my companions in the mineral kingdom – Oh Shinnah and Dhyani Ywahoo.

Thanks also to Guy Saint-Jean, who knew how to provide the resources required to realise this book, and to Micheline Fraser for the transcription and corrections.

And thanks also to all those who have worked in collaboration with me so that Pédagogies Alternatives can pass on these teachings.

Luc Bourgault

PREFACE

༄

The text that follows is an adaptation, by the author Luc Bourgault, of the records from his two courses on *The American Indian's Approach to the Use of Crystals in Therapy*. The teachings have, until quite recently, always been passed on by word of mouth, in line with the didactic tradition particular to the American Indians of the Cherokee and Apache tribes.

The traditions of the American Indians call upon the synchronisation of the two hemispheres of the brain (a concept also known as self-focusing), in order to achieve a full and complete understanding of the teachings. Two pedagogical techniques, amongst others, help this synchronisation, be it in a ritual or ceremonial context, as does the repetition of the teaching.

With the oral teaching, in the courses given by Luc Bourgault, each day starts with an opening ceremony – a time for prayer and silence – where invocation of the spirits and purification of the site are the prelude to a chant of welcome, which everyone sings together. This acts as a greeting for the participants and allows them to focus themselves. The author advises all his pupils to attend more than one session because, by its very nature, oral teaching is never exactly the same on each occasion. By hearing the same information in a different context, one can grasp it as a whole, thus encouraging a more comprehensive and complete understanding.

The writing of a book such as this one poses its own questions. In a traditional context, such a book would be useless and even counter-productive. The reason that the author has now decided to commit these teachings to writing – and that his elders have given him permission to do so – is so that he can actually help to advance the open-minded attitude of the 'New Age', in particular with what is referred to as the 'power of the crystal'.

Unfortunately, a great amount of the information that

has been disseminated in the current wave of popularity is incorrect and contradictory. Some of the techniques described in certain books are even harmful and could be dangerous for those who try them. Among these, there are two practices in particular which could be seriously disturbing:

• placing crystals on the ground in a geometric configuration and sitting in the middle to meditate;

• placing crystals directly on one's energy centres (chakras). This practice is particularly dangerous when carried out on several chakras with a number of crystals.

What is more, the techniques described in such books can often be harmful to the crystals themselves. For example, the practice of leaving a crystal in sea salt for several hours creates holes in the etheric tissue that surrounds the mineral beings.

The gift of working with crystals is not bestowed on everyone. A spiritual process of purification and clarification is essential and, without this, a crystal can be of more harm than good. The misuse of crystals on a large scale actually damages the delicate ecological balance of the Earth, which has already been seriously impaired.

For all these reasons, the author decided to make basic information regarding therapeutic work with crystals generally available. This book could not and does not aim to provide a complete and adequate training in crystal therapy. For that, it is essential that the teaching is given verbally and the practice supervised. However, in shedding light on the fundamental principles, this book should be helpful for those who already use crystals. For those new to the subject, it should also uncover some of the mysteries of this thousand-year-old science which is still of immense value to us in our lives today.

CONTENTS

PROLOGUE

My name is Luc Bourgault Blue Eagle Ousti Catoui. I work as a teacher, giving courses throughout Quebec in Canada. I teach the therapeutic use of crystals, according to the American Indian approach, and musical therapy as well as American Indian spirituality. I am also a lecturer, ecologist, writer, musician and occasional poet.

My life with crystals goes back to my childhood. I began to be interested in them when I was very young – in fact, from the age of five.

One day, when I was returning home from school, I came across this particular stone in the street. It was of clear quartz and as big as my father's fist. I found it very beautiful, a translucent rock through which one could see. I had never seen one before. I took it back to my bedroom and placed it on a small stool in such a way that the light from the sun shone through the crystal. I sat down in front of it and began meditating.

After about five minutes, the room around me disappeared: there was just me and the crystal floating in an indefinable space. I felt wonderful. Shortly after that, time seemed to stand still and I was in a state of complete bliss.

I don't think that it lasted very long. I decided to 'come back' to my room so that I could go out and play. At that age we are all still close to our origins and such things are only natural. I did not see anything special in what had happened.

I was happily playing outside when I felt as if someone was pulling me upwards by my hair. I started running and rushed straight to my room. The crystal had gone. The sun still shone on the same spot and the stool was still in the same place, but the stone had disappeared. I asked my mother if she had touched the crystal or if someone else had been in my room. She assured me that nobody had been in there.

Ever since then, each time I come across a similar white rock, I pick it up – even now.

When I was nine I joined the Lapidary Club at Saskatoon University in Saskatchewan. I saw some beautiful stones there, but the club did not have what I was really looking for. The approach to stones was basically a scientific one and no one ever spoke about them in the way that I felt.

I also tried my hand at selling stones. Being young, I went knocking on doors with my small white rocks – a cent each. When anyone did not want to buy, I would look at them through a stone and, wishing as hard as I could, I would say: 'You must have this stone'. All of a sudden it worked and the person bought one.

Some years later my family moved to Quebec. Obviously the boxes of rock I had accumulated during my childhood did not come with me and for a few years I forgot all about the mineral world.

Following my studies at university, and having travelled round Canada and the United States, I realised that, having lived among the American Indians, I just had to work with them. On my return to Montreal in 1980, my yoga teacher told me that an American Indian woman – a Cherokee (*Tsalagi* in autochthonous language) named Dhyani Ywahoo, who was a faith healer and priestess in America – was coming to Montreal to give a lecture.

I went to the lecture and finally discovered there the spiritual nourishment for which I had been searching. I had travelled among the American Indians, but while I learned a lot through my contact with the Autochthones on the reserves and in the city centres, it was not specifically the 'wise men' that I met. I had also noticed several social problems, one of which was alcoholism – an area of discussion both friendly and explosive. So this Cherokee woman was the first I had encountered who had both wisdom and knowledge.

The evening was electric. I took in every word she said. During the talk, she unfastened a crystal that she was wearing on her dress and began energising it with her hands while she was speaking. At the end of the lecture, she passed it to her assistant and left. The latter came straight up to me and said: 'This crystal is for you'. As I received it, I felt a charge of energy so great that I could not speak any more. Then the assistant asked me: 'Is the crystal yours?' Since I was unable to speak, I put it in my mouth. She saw then that it was indeed mine.

The next evening, I had a vision which later gave me the name that I now carry – Blue Eagle.

As a result, I studied with Dhyani Ywahoo for several years and still do. She only teaches those people already well versed in the subject as she believes that crystals are more volatile than the atomic bomb. In the tradition of her people, only certain chosen ones are able to work with crystals, and they must meditate for several years before even being able to touch the stones. Crystals are very powerful because they amplify energy. If someone is impure and their thoughts and emotions are also impure, crystals will amplify those forces which will then become harmful.

One day in 1988 I saw a photo of Oh Shinnah Fastwolf in a magazine. It advertised a workshop she was running, for a week in Colorado, on the therapeutic use of crystals. As soon as I saw her face I knew I had to go there. At the time I was already giving some courses on crystals, thanks to the clairvoyance I had developed. I was using a 'New Age' book that I felt then was good, but I relied above all on my instinct and meditation when working with crystals.

However, following my week of studies with Oh Shinnah, I had to reject part of what I had formulated from this method. I acquired a healthy mistrust for what are known as 'New Age' techniques, which has lasted ever since, and I gained confidence in the teachings of Oh Shinnah, because they had proved themselves.

Oh Shinnah is from the Teneh tribe (also called Apache) and enjoys a powerful ancestral heritage in several traditions. Her grandmother was a Mohawk and a theosophist and, as such, very close to both European and American Indian esoteric thought. Belonging to the Teneh tribe, Oh Shinnah became learned in all the sophisticated and deep-rooted knowledge of crystals that is particular to this tribe.

There are two American Indian tribes that have truly what one calls the 'Priest Craft Tradition' – the Tsalagis and the Tenehs. In these tribes, they train people, chosen with the aim of becoming faith healers and priests. With other tribes, it is shamanism which prevails, where individuals receive their shaman power from someone else or gain it through illness or other circumstances in life.

The Tsalagis and Tenehs are among the only American Indian tribes to provide certain chosen people with a training in prayer, meditation, healing and ceremony. They are also the only tribes to have really developed the therapeutic use of crystals and they are careful to train individuals thoroughly before allowing them to use the crystals.

Oh Shinnah holds a degree in experimental psychology. She has worked in several American institutions and alongside scientists who have carried out research in their laboratories on her work and knowledge. She has therefore been in a position to verify with them, by means of scientific experiments, the use of crystals in therapy and to prove the scientific value of the ancestral techniques with which she works. This has given her a certain credibility among those surgeons, doctors, psychiatrists, psychologists and nurses who have studied with her.

In the United States today there are thousands of such health practitioners using the techniques with crystals, expounded by Oh Shinnah Fastwolf. There is even an American surgeon who will not accept any patient on his operating table if there is not a crystal in the room. He has noticed that the period of the patient's convalescence is reduced by a third when he uses a crystal in surgery. He does not understand why or how this works, but he is obliged to accept the facts and always uses one.

Certain care units in those American hospitals which have been prepared to experiment, have taken note of the therapeutic power of crystals and now keep some in a bowl of salted water, which the nurses use regularly. A well-known New York psychiatrist works with these same techniques by means of egg-shaped crystals and stones. He places one of them on the patient's chair so that before sitting down, the patient quite naturally picks up the stone and holds on to it throughout the consultation. Now the psychiatrist complains that his patients are being cured too quickly and that he is losing money.

We have checked on the truth of these techniques and I would advise everyone to do the same. Do not accept blindly what you are told. Verify for yourself the results that you obtain with the use of crystals. Having seen for yourself, you will have faith and your work will be a lot stronger, because you will be doing it with conviction. This is important when you are providing help. The person who approaches you for assistance will be able to rely on this power that you have acquired, through a balanced knowledge of the techniques you employ.

Oh Shinnah taught me certain techniques that I am not going to touch on in this book, simply because I have not yet tried them. There is a wealth of knowledge and experimentation that still awaits me.

The most important thing to remember is that experience, life and feeling are fundamental. Whatever you try to do in life, the two hemispheres of the brain should always be involved – that is to say, you must use both knowledge and experience.

Finally, I want to stress the fact that the majority of the teachings I will be offering here on the therapeutic use of crystals come from Oh Shinnah of the Teneh tribe.

INTRODUCTION

℘

There are two basic principles which anyone who wants to work with crystals must understand – meditation and respect.

MEDITATION

To begin with, the first crystal with which you work, which you clean, polish and purify, must be yourself. It is an illusion to think that you can work effectively with crystals if you have not already started the work on your own self. You must recognise that this work you do on yourself is the most important work of all.

Even if you have plenty of success, power or material well-being, you will have to leave it all behind you when you die and, if you have not worked on yourself, you will be back to square one. You will have accomplished nothing, despite all your wealth.

When you work on yourself, you acquire a richness that is eternal and that does not disappear with death.

'... Men die, but are reborn in the real world of the Great-Hope, where there exists only the spirits of everything; and we are able to know this true life here on earth if we purify our bodies and our souls, thus bringing us closer to the Great-Hope which is All-Purity.'
Héhaka Sapa, The Secret Rites of the Sioux Indians, Paris PRP, 1975, p 65.

Working on yourself gives you the feeling of having really achieved something, and this follows you right into your next life. Indeed, meditation should be the first thing taught in schools. It is the beginning of work on oneself. Thanks to meditation, we can start to control the crystals that we are.

Because, in effect, we are crystals. The blood and fluids that make up our body are, on the whole, liquid crystals. Water, at the heart of the living biological body, is largely composed of liquid crystals (Patrick and Gael Flanagan, *Elixir of the Ageless*, Flagstaff, Arizona, Vortex Press, 1986, p 37.). Among certain very enlightened people, one can find crystals which have formed themselves just under the skull.

So it is vital that you first work on yourself.

There is one thing that you can be sure of when working with crystals and that is change. But it is impossible to know in advance how this change will take place. When you set out on a spiritual path – and if you are sincere – you must often face up to a number of tests. For example, at the moment when you settle down to meditate, you may be disturbed by such everyday events as the telephone ringing incessantly or noisy children interrupting you. The spirit wants to check if we are really sincere in our approach. Such tests enable us to cultivate perseverance and stability.

We must never forget that crystals are amplifiers and transformers of energy. The least thought or gesture is immediately enlarged by the crystal. This is why it is so important that we work on purifying and controlling ourselves – mastering the ego so that we can achieve the greatest well-being in all our relationships. If we are not working on ourselves, we should not be working with crystals.

The principal criticism I have of many books on sale today is that they omit this great truth: that you must work on yourself before even touching a crystal. You must understand that the crystal is a tool. It is not the crystal which will do the work but the person who holds it and who channels their will to heal into it.

So, if you have not adopted from the start a certain spiritual approach – that is to say, if you do not purify the crystal that is you – it is wrong to believe you will obtain beneficial results from crystal therapy.

Meditation, prayer and physical exercises are all appropriate means of achieving purification of, and control over, one's thoughts, feelings, words and gestures. Meditation is essential, whether one is talking of discipline, practice or the spiritual path.

I favour specific forms of meditation – those of the American Indians – because they are in tune with the natural rhythms of the earth. However, the choice of how you meditate does not necessarily influence the result you will obtain. Often, the meditation and prayers we should use, to begin with, are those that our parents used before us.

Equally, when one feels in harmony with a group of people who are praying, it is of little importance how they do it. Energy always manifests itself, whether one is attending a Catholic Mass or an American Indian, Buddhist or Hindu ceremony. The same truths are being expressed and the fact of praying in a group manifests this potential and purifies intentions. Prayer acts not only on those united in praying but also, at an environmental level, on all those around us. For example, in my study of Tibetan Buddhism I have discovered there the same principles that I first learned from American Indian spirituality.

Certain forms of meditation are almost identical. At the end of the day, the important thing is to have a spiritual discipline, never mind which, as long as you are happy with it.

You must have somewhere you can go each day, to sit down quietly and consider your thoughts. Without judging these thoughts, you can see for yourself how you think, how you react and what your feelings and emotions are. When, and only when, you can distinguish all these thoughts, can you have any influence over them.

This influence does not necessarily consist in taking a decision, but more in seeing clearly. Once you are able to see clearly, you will not repeat your mistakes. It is not always necessary to want to change. Often it is sufficient simply to see with clarity in order to change. If you realise, for example, that you are thinking badly about someone, you should concentrate on the antidote – that is, the opposite thought. But if you are not sufficiently attentive to realise that you have had that bad thought in the first place, it will continue to follow its course.

It is important to understand that we are like a great lake, where all our thoughts are waves which reach many people before touching the shore and returning to us. Thus, if you have a bad thought about someone, it will touch that person and subsequently come back to you. You must therefore be very careful about what you think.

The following proverbs are prominent in American Indian spirituality: 'One should never speak badly about people' and 'One should never talk about their bad sides', because to do so amplifies these negative aspects. Not only to think such negative thoughts but also to say them aloud, encourages this negativity twice over.

By contrast, here is an example of what is recommended.

When the white man arrived, the Cherokees gave him a name: 'the man who seems to be evil' but not 'the man who is evil'. The reason for this was to give him the chance to change, to give him room to be able to transform if he wanted to stop behaving as he was doing and become different. The Cherokees did not reinforce the white man's behaviour through their thoughts and negative words. They noted his behaviour but without going as far as thinking he was irredeemably like that.

You should also be aware that your body contains a number of channels. The grandparents and teachers of Dhyani Ywahoo all lived to the age of about 125, because the channels in their body remained open throughout their lives. It would be wrong to think that they became immobile in their final years. In fact, right up until death they were still supple, their backs still straight, and they even danced every morning.

While all the channels in your body are open, your cells receive sufficient food. A cell that is adequately nourished is almost eternal (Patrick and Gael Flanagan, *Elixir of the Ageless*, Flagstaff, Arizona, Vortex Press, 1986, p 37.). It regenerates continuously, provided that it is well fed. When you meditate, you start first by opening the channels inside your body. Once that is done, you are in harmony with all that lives in the universe.

We are all, everyone and everything, interrelated. In our culture, we have a tendency to separate things, whether it is scientific disciplines, different classes of people or children of different ages and stages of learning at school. We put up fences to divide our land from that of others, then barriers, then frontiers. Finally, we adopt a separatist mental approach, forgetting that we are all interrelated.

We cannot entirely dissociate ourselves from our environment however, because if we damage the ecology of the Earth, it will turn against us. This interrelationship is continual. We must pay great attention to our thoughts and our words, because they are the bricks with which we build our tomorrows. The life we live is the result of our thoughts, our words and our actions, and these always come from our thoughts. Before drawing up any plans, the architect must stop to consider what type of house he is trying to create.

Likewise, we must be careful about what we think, if we aim to create harmony around us.

I must stress the importance of sitting down at least twice a day, with your spinal column upright towards the sky, and rediscovering yourself in an atmosphere of silence. It is excellent for your health, because the energy that is not being used up in looking, listening, feeling, tasting or speaking returns to the inside of your being and revives you.

At the same time, the channels inside your body purify themselves, thus allowing you to start seeing who you really are. There is a great richness in knowing who you really are, what your potential is and what you have to work with. When you stop to meditate, you will discover that there exists inside you a great mystery, a deep source which connects you with the universe. The same exists in all of us and, from this, love and compassion will be born. Then we can approach others in all sincerity and help them.

Meditation and work on yourself, these must provide the basis of your efforts before you attempt to use crystals. Your spiritual path will take you everywhere in life. Do not look any further. The essential is there. You are more than a body, more than a personality, more than a name. You are a divine source, identical to that which some call Allah, the Great-Spirit or God.

Some autochthonous nations give this divine source the name of 'Great Mystery', because it is, in fact, inside us all and too expansive to be named or described. While you work on your meditation, you could compare yourself with an onion. Quietly, you shed your outer layers to arrive at the heart, the divine source which connects you to everything.

The first principle is therefore: the first crystal with which I must work is myself.

RESPECT

The second principle is respect. You can understand this when you realise that crystals are living beings and an intimate part of the Earth. Scientists often consider the Earth as a globe of land, of stones and of water which floats in space, when in fact it is a person, an entity, a being of very great evolution.

Dhyani Ywahoo's grandmother is reincarnated into the planetary system, because she had been through all the experience that she had to acquire on this Earth. Today she is a much more expansive being, able to welcome a number of forms of life and help a multitude of beings, in a way that she could not when she was just a human being. She has passed through another stage of evolution and has become a planet.

Mother Earth, as the American Indians call her, is a being of very great evolution which actually suffers enormously because she has been forgotten by her children – that is to say, you and me. We have forgotten that she is a living being and that she needs our prayers, just as she needs our respect, in the same way as our biological mother.

We have taken everything from her to satisfy our own greed without worrying about what will remain for the generations to come. We shave the Earth's hair (forests) right down to the soil. We have exploded atomic bombs in her stomach, thus provoking earth shocks that have shifted the North Pole by three or four metres. Equally, we suck out her hormones (oil) to run our cars and heat our homes and we pollute her blood (the waters of the earth) and her lungs (the atmosphere).

Thus we are creating a major imbalance in the body of Mother Earth. At the moment, the etheric heart of the earth is in the process of shifting.

With the rotation of the Earth, there are four states: the stable state, that of transient sliding ('slippage'), that of constant sliding ('wobble') and finally the state of spinning or rapid rotation ('spin'). This last state has already been noted in the history of the planet, when it left its orbit at the time of the great ice ages.

We are currently in the third state, that of constant sliding. If we allow ourselves to enter the next state, the one in which the Earth spins on itself and leaves its orbit, we will disappear completely. Everything will be flattened and frozen across the whole of the planet.

Before reaching this state, we must stop our wicked actions throughout the world and learn once again to respect it. Every one of us has a responsibility towards it. We have to understand that we are the Earth's conscience. Humanity has the intelligence necessary to bring about a change, in the same way as it had the means to bring about the ecological disaster towards which we are heading today.

Above all, we must not wait for governments to take

action, since they themselves are the source of the serious environmental problems with which we are faced, through the excessive use of technology for economic ends. Economics has led to a system in which everyone takes for themselves, without worrying about others. Some never stop accumulating wealth, while their neighbours have nothing and die from poverty. This never used to happen. People shared amongst themselves and also with the animal, vegetable and mineral kingdoms, with Mother Earth, with the winds and the clouds. All are animated by the spirit, are alive and have a conscience.

When I hold my courses in the heart of the country, some people are surprised by the response from the elements. For example, the weather improves as we begin and lasts up to the start of meditation. Then it rains until we finish meditating. It rains non-stop during meditation because I ask for that. Then I make an offering, asking for fine weather, and shortly afterwards the sun shines. Each time it is the same.

When one learns to communicate with the elements, a kind of synchronisation is set up. It is not me who makes it rain or brings on the sunshine, but the elements which want to respond to my prayers, because I am in harmony with them.

Certain events are often quoted in the American Indian tradition, such as the following:

An enormous drought had been going on for months. An Indian arrived and was asked if he could make the rain come. He prayed and half an hour later it began to rain. But the people there would have been able to do the same, because thanks are the food of the gods. We must give thanks for what we have.

If you eat every day, who gives you the food? It is nature, Mother Earth in her great goodness. If you do not thank her, you are being disrespectful. If we continue to behave in this way, what has been given to us will in some way be taken away. The day will come when our society, having taken everything without any consideration for nature, will suffer from hunger for having misused the natural resources and for not having shown due consideration towards other forms of life on the planet.

We have therefore, each one of us, a responsibility for the ecological calamity we face. We all have a relationship with the environment and are responsible for our own existence and the pollution we create. We must be very conscious of all that if we want to use crystals, which are also tools of communication. Everything that we think, say and do is registered, expressed and amplified by the crystals.

If you possess a power such as that of working with crystals, you have also the responsibility for it. With any power there comes responsibility.

Crystals are the eyes, the ears, the nose and the mouth of the Earth, which uses them to see, to hear, to smell and to taste. It is also through them that it communicates with its other brothers and sisters, with other planets in the solar system. Each crystal taken from the Earth maintains its contact with the heart of the Earth. In many ways crystals are a little like 'the eye of God', communicating to the heavens and the Earth the thoughts and actions of humanity.

There are, in the cosmos, superior hierarchies to the human being which, by means of the crystal, come to test our planet. It goes without saying that we are, at the moment, regarded very unfavourably. Man has often made lamentable mistakes in using crystals and, if people like Dhyani did not exist to communicate with these superior hierarchies and speak up in our defence, we would have been wiped out a long time ago.

For all these reasons, we must be very meticulous about the way in which we use crystals.

We must also be careful about how we react, day by day, towards the environment. Rather than throwing paper away in the bin, we must collect and recycle it. We must do the same with metal, plastic and glass. If the selective collection of household rubbish has not been organised in your area, get together and put pressure on those responsible to arrange it. You must act and do something for the ecology of the Earth. It is your responsibility.

Future generations depend on our choices, our decisions and our deeds. What kind of world are we keeping for those who follow? Will the air be clean enough to breathe and the water clean enough to drink? We must think about this – and act. Just one person conscious of his or her responsibility can make a great difference and if you work with crystals, you will have an additional power to bring about changes.

It is very important to think about the health of Mother Earth when working with crystals, because one is manipulating some very private parts of her body. She is quite happy to accept this form of crystalline life, so one must respect it by respecting each crystal, which belongs to her body. Significantly, the American Indians call stones and crystals 'the bones of Mother Earth'.

The second principle is therefore: respect.

Understanding these two basic principles will provide a favourable foundation on which it will be possible to create an effective and balanced therapy that respects the laws of the universe. You must take whatever time is required to do the work well. The mighty oak did not grow up in a day. It is more important to walk the right path than to try running along it in the hope of reaching the destination more quickly.

Everything in its time, one step at a time, slowly but surely. This is the natural way, the way that teaches life. As Dhyani put it so clearly, the important thing is to meditate, to contemplate the nature of our spirit. The mystery and powers that manifest themselves are thus secondary. The true conquest lies in understanding ourselves, in seeing that our thoughts, words and deeds shape our lives, the world around us and the generations to come.

PURIFICATION AND CARE OF CRYSTALS

❧

I now want to talk about purification and care of crystals, since these techniques are among the most important in any work with crystals. Before beginning any work with your crystals it is a good idea to purify the room in which you will be working.

The American Indians always burn some sage, cedarwood or scented hay for purifying. They do this, for example, before making love, holding a meeting or going hunting. They will purify the room in which they are sleeping, in order to have beautiful dreams, or a patient's electromagnetic field before starting the healing process.

Oh Shinnah wanted to verify this purification technique in a laboratory and find out why all the North American tribes adopted this procedure. She noticed that the smoke from those three herbs (sage, cedarwood and scented hay) had the potential of seizing the positive ion in the air molecule and extracting it. That is why you must never forget to open a window when burning these herbs. If there is no opening, you will not really be able to drive the harmful elements out of the room and change the force, because there will be nowhere for them to escape to.

The positive ion in the air molecule is the electric charge that is harmful for your health. You come across it in places that are heavily polluted or that have been closed for a long time without air. On the other hand, the negative ion is beneficial for your health. After an electric storm it exists in abundance, because the flashes of lightning free thousands of millions of negative ions into the air. This is why the air is so invigorating following a storm.

Negative ions are present in great quantities in coniferous forests and above or near the sea. Nowadays you can buy air purifiers which generate these ions and are able to cut down pollution. The negative ions cancel out the positive ones, which keep pollution suspended in the air until it finally settles on the ground or surrounding surfaces. Therefore, you can see the accumulation of dirt on the walls and objects around these air purifiers.

The American Indian incense (sage, cedarwood and scented hay) also takes away the positive ions and leaves only negative ions. So there is scientific proof that when you burn sage, cedarwood or scented hay, you drive away the undesirable ions or 'bad spirits'.

I would suggest that all forces of a heavy, harmful or maleficent nature need a vehicle on which to be carried and this vehicle is the positive ion that one finds in the air molecule. Such forces as envy, jealousy, anger and hate use positive ions to breed. It is therefore very beneficial for your environment to adopt the habit of burning this incense. You can use just one plant or a mixture of two or all three of the plants mentioned. My students and I use it regularly, at least twice a day. Before meditating in the morning and the evening, we always burn this incense.

With each treatment, during consultation with a patient, it is the first thing that you should do. Normally the person is standing up and you burn the incense around him, starting by the feet and lifting it up in front of him as far as the head and then doing the same behind him. This way, his electromagnetic field will appear clearer, since you will have administered an initial purification, and the operation will be made easier. Whatever the patient has experienced that day will be removed and you yourself will not pick up the forces that are driven out of him during the purification and therapy.

You must understand that if you want to be happy and have power in your life, you must be in harmony with the Earth on which you live. For thousands of years geographical harmonies have been established with the spiritual world. Because of this, the spirit responds to certain things, in certain places, according to these harmonies.

When you move into a new home, it is the first thing you must do – and the same goes for your existing home if you have not already purified it. The people who lived there before you have released thoughts and emotions about which you know nothing. Even the timber or bricks, at the time when the house was built, have been permeated by the vibrant influence of the workmen.

You must start the purification process by opening a door and a window in each room. Then begin by the open door and follow the perimeter of the wall. In this way, you will inevitably return to the same place, but from the other side. Burn the incense, making sure you go into every corner since different forces often remain trapped here. In olden times, houses were sometimes round or conical in shape, which enabled forces to circulate better, because the form that force naturally takes is the spiral. Do not forget items like wardrobes, cupboards and drawers. When you have finished, close the windows.

In general, it is good to purify your home every three or four months. On subsequent occasions, it will not be necessary to treat the rooms in such minute detail. You need only spend longer in those rooms you frequent the most or where you meditate or carry out any treatment.

On the majority of occasions that I stay in a hotel bed-room, I feel strange forces there. So I always carry out this practice of purifying. I light the incense, open the door and window and walk right round the room. When I have finished, the forces are neutralised and I feel at ease there. It is very effective and I urge you to do the same.

I always burn the incense in a natural shell – traditionally an abalone shell. I still use this today since it is very heat-resistant, but it does not matter what type of shell you have. In addition to being a natural, unchanged object, the shell symbolises the element water. In the alchemic process of change during fumigation, the four elements are all represented. The shell comes from the sea, the match that lights the incense is the fire, the herbs and cedar are the earth and the smoke is the air.

There is just one technique for purifying crystals and that has been verified scientifically, under laboratory conditions, by Oh Shinnah. First you need a bowl made of natural material (glass, ceramic, stoneware, wood, etc.). Avoid using plastic or metal. Pour either natural source or distilled water into the bowl and add a pinch of sea salt (the exact proportion being a quarter of a teaspoon per litre of water).

It is a good idea to keep this bowl near your bed, because you will see later how important it is to purify your crystals every day. You will be able, for example, to put your jewellery into the bowl before you go to bed and take out the crystal with which you sleep. The following morning, you can remove your jewellery and put your night crystal back in the bowl.

You should use the same method to purify every new stone or crystal that you get (whether it is a jewel or simply a stone) for a whole week – seven days and seven nights. This operation will ensure that its memory, former programming and positive ions, which have been able to accumulate around the electromagnetic field of the crystal, are completely purified.

The crystal has a very extensive memory. It remembers all the places it has been, all the people who have touched it and all the forces that have impregnated it. It is its molecular structure which gives it this particularity. Indeed, as you may know, minute pieces of crystal are used as 'chips' in computers and act as their memory.

In order to be able to work successfully with your crystal, you must purify it properly, since you want to know exactly what forces it amplifies, what 'memories' it contains. For therapy, you must not work with just any old force, without knowing which. You must therefore erase the crystal's memory by placing it for a whole week in the solution of salted water.

This technique of purifying crystals is dependent on an electrical phenomenon. The crystals of sea salt which are dissolved are distributed equally among the molecules of water and create an electric charge in each molecule of water, which is stronger than that present in the molecules of crystal. This causes the memory of the crystal to be erased and the positive ions which accumulate in its electromagnetic field to be released, thus making it ready for therapeutic use.

I once knew a man who wore a quartz crystal around his neck near his throat. This man always had a sore throat. When I discovered that he had not purified the crystal, I advised him to take it off and 15 minutes later his sore throat had disappeared. He probably had some discordant thoughts or intentions which were registered in the crystal and so his throat remained sore all the time he wore it round his neck.

As you can see, it can be damaging for one's health to wear crystals that have not been correctly purified. And to do this, one only has to soak them for 20 minutes in salted water – the time it takes to have a shower, for example.

A crystal that is worn for protection or therapeutic reasons must be purified every day. A static crystal, which is placed on a table, desk or other piece of furniture and remains there, does not need to be purified quite so often. Every three weeks or so is sufficient. Let your intuition be your guide.

A crystal that is being used for therapy must be purified after each treatment. You can check on the truth of this by carrying out a little test. Choose three or four of your precious stones, crystals or jewellery, that you have been purifying for a week. Then compare them with your other jewellery. You will notice that those that have been purified shine more and have more light than those that have not been purified.

Let us now deal with the maintenance or care of crystals.

In the same way as you need a holiday, an outing or a change of air, crystals also need to recharge themselves. They particularly like running water, a stream, a small river or, as a last resort, being put under a tap. Afterwards, they appear very happy and shine like a thousand fires. It is one of the ways they have of expressing themselves, through the phenomenon of light.

Every so often try to leave your crystals for an hour or two in running water, making sure that they will not be carried away by the current. You can also use tap water, particularly if this is supplied from a natural source such as a well. Put the crystals on a natural surface (wood, for example) and let the water run over them.

We know that crystals are very hard, which makes them impact-resistant. That is why we use them as jewellery. However, if they are struck at a certain angle, especially in their natural state, they can break like glass. Two crystals can also scratch each other and, when one crystal is in contact with another, they can exchange forces or programmes.

In order to avoid any of this happening, you should wrap each crystal individually in some natural red fabric. This fabric can be 100 per cent cotton, linen, silk or wool, for example, but you must always use natural fibres since crystals do not like synthetic fabrics. The colour red is specified because it has the slowest rate of absorption of luminous vibrations and is the most resistant. As such, it forms a kind of natural energy barrier, preventing the crystal from receiving outside forces or, in its turn, giving off its own programme.

For example, if you hold a crystal that has been programmed to enhance concentration when your intention is to relax yourself, it is important that you are not influenced by its programming. If the crystal is wrapped in a red fabric then this will contain the programme. In the same way, if you are carrying some crystals that are, from an energy point of view, fragile (for some ceremonial or personal use), you must protect them from the energy of other people. It is therefore important to keep your crystals wrapped in red fabric and protected from outside forces.

I have actually had the chance to verify the efficacy of this technique for myself. On the first few occasions that I went to exhibitions to buy crystals, I found it most disturbing. I was in an enormous room, right in the middle of numerous stands offering a multitude of crystals that had not been purified. Because these were all jumbled up together, the forces were very harmful. As I was particularly sensitive to these forces, I became very nervous and hyperactive. Despite the fascination I had for all these stones, I had an overwhelming urge to run from the room.

As a result, I made some bad purchases. Realising what had happened, I wanted to put matters right and went back, but this time dressed from head to foot in red cotton. I was able to make my purchases calmly, without suffering from the internal stress I had felt before, except perhaps for the looks people gave me for the way I was clothed.

This experience proved to me the efficacy of red cotton as a protection against the exchange of crystalline energy.

It is useful to wrap your crystals in a natural red fabric when carrying them about or when you are not using them. On the other hand, if you are wearing a crystal around your neck or in your pocket and you want its vibrations to help you, you must keep it unwrapped, so that its influence will not be contained by the fabric.

Certain books stipulate that you must put crystals in natural salt in order to purify them. Such a practice is harmful for the crystals since it creates a hole in their electromagnetic field. If you have done this by mistake, you can rectify the situation however.

First you must apologise to the crystal, because you must never forget that it is a living being. Then you must bury it in the ground for 24 hours, which will enable it to use the telluric forces to recover its electromagnetic field. Finally, you must purify it for a week in salted water.

Some other books recommend exposing crystals to sunlight in order to energise them. For some crystals, perhaps, this is true. The sun acts like a universal battery, the source of all energy in the world of physics. On the other hand, certain crystals do not like this solar energy because they have grown up in the earth, sheltered from any light, and so the sun hits them too violently.

In any event, you do not have to put your crystals in sunlight to energise them. It is enough simply to put them in some running water, such as I have already mentioned. Only where your objective is to programme a crystal with solar energy should you expose it to sunlight.

Finally, you must establish a good relationship with your crystal, one of friendship. It is alive and aware of your presence. Show it respect, as you must do towards all forms of life. Do not think in terms of using it, but rather of working with it. You can, on occasions, while you are meditating, allow the smoke from cedarwood to pass over it before communicating with it, heart to heart. Thank it for its help and follow carefully the instructions that I have already given.

If you do all this, you will gain a friend who will work wholeheartedly to help you.

STONES AND
THEIR PROPERTIES

What actually is a crystal? It is a mineral substance, the molecular composition of which is arranged and geometrically fixed in space. That is to say, the molecules are structured in a geometric way, some well aligned against others. This phenomenon can be seen with the naked eye since the crystal's molecular structure is visible from the outside.

When you look at a crystal, you can see faces, angles, geometric planes and sometimes a point. It is a reflection of the geometric order which exists on the molecular plane. When the mineral substance reveals its crystalline structure, through visible geometric forms, we call it a crystal. It is this arranged structure of molecules which gives the crystal its properties as an amplifier and transformer of energy.

There are some micro-crystalline substances, such as agates and jaspers, which also contain molecular structures geometrically organised in space. Unlike crystals, however, their form is not visible to the naked eye and they appear to be ordinary stones without geometric form. Only under a microscope is it possible to see the thousands of little crystals of which they are composed.

Other substances are also used for therapy which are neither crystalline nor micro-crystalline, such as coral and turquoise. But essentially it is crystalline and micro-crystalline minerals that are used.

CLEAR QUARTZ

In therapy, certain types of crystal are used more than others. Clear quartz, which is pure light, is one of them. It gives us the impression of being a solid substance, although in fact it vibrates with frequencies which surpass our actual comprehension. It is one of the most perfect forms in the known universe.

From the two qualities of light and perfection flow the properties which one uses in therapy. Anything that is thick, heavy, wicked or hurtful cannot pass through the crystal, because that which is pure light is contrary to darkness. Likewise, all that is hatred, jealousy, envy, anger and so on cannot pass through the crystal either. This constitutes a protection which repels any physical attack, aberration, possession or force that is harmful and contrary to your electromagnetic field.

When you use a quartz crystal for protection, for example, to repel from your electromagnetic field anything you find harmful, you should wear it on your 'spiritual' plexus. So named by Oh Shinnah, this is situated at the point of the breastbone, between the solar plexus and the cardiac plexus. It is, in fact, the most sensitive part of the human body. It is through the spiritual plexus that we receive all the impressions, feelings and emotions that come from without, for example, the force of someone's anger when it is directed against us.

Therefore, to protect your electromagnetic field, it is advisable to wear a clear quartz crystal on your spiritual plexus.

Another particular characteristic of the clear quartz crystal is its light refraction index, which is 1.55 (signifying that it bends the luminous zones at an angle of 1.55 degrees). As it works with the light, you should not wear the protective crystal inside your clothes and hidden from the light, but always on the outside. In this way, a dark or negative force will automatically be dispelled by the effect of the light and the amplification of your electromagnetic field produced by the quartz crystal.

You must be very careful as to exactly where you wear your crystal. A number of people are inclined to wear it a little higher up than the spiritual plexus, probably for aesthetic reasons, but at this height the crystal does not protect.

The following anecdote illustrates the protective effect of the crystal:

I was exhibiting at a show and a crowd of people passed in front of my stand throughout the course of the day. One person working with me was very sensitive to the forces of others and she became overwhelmed by the sheer mass of different forces. These sensations grew so unbearable that she had to go outside regularly and, as the day went by, she was forced to leave the hall more and more frequently.

To remedy this situation, I took a small pendant of quartz crystal and put it round her neck. The crystal hung just over her spiritual plexus. From that moment on, she was able to remain on the stand for five hours non-stop. All the forces from the people who passed by were immediately pushed away from her electromagnetic field and thus she was able to face the public for the whole of the day without being overwhelmed.

You will notice for yourself, when you are similarly protected, that you feel a lot more relaxed and happy to approach others. At the end of the day you will feel less exhausted because you will have been less affected by those around you. People who work with the public can help to reduce their stress levels by wearing clear quartz.

Crystals that are natural or shaped in a natural form with six faces and a point should be worn with their point facing down towards the ground in a way that 'earths' your energy. If you wear a crystal with the point upwards, it will tend to accumulate energy at the level of your throat chakra. You will feel your throat dry up and sometimes have difficulty in speaking. Moreover, you will have a tendency to retain undesirable forces, because they will have less chance of draining down into the ground where their effect will be nullified.

The other extremity of the crystal must be kept free. Any silver or gold added to hold the crystal, when it is being used as a piece of jewellery, must not completely cover up the area opposite the point. The mounting must pass round the crystal, allowing it to breathe through this end as well as through its point. Some crystals are completely covered at the opposite end to the point with a silver or gold alloy. In this case, they are unable to breathe properly.

The majority of shaped crystals today have a point at both ends. These are less efficient than those which have just a single point directed towards the ground. However, clear quartz can be shaped in a variety of forms and it is not necessary for it to have a point and six sides.

It is essential to purify every day a crystal that you wear for protection. You must also try to prevent other people touching it because, if they do, they will put a charge of positive ions into the crystal, which will block it up and make it less efficient.

A particular quality of quartz crystal is its ability to attract positive ions and release negative ions, a process which is beneficial for the body.

People are naturally attracted to crystals and sometimes, before you have a chance to prevent them, they may reach out and touch the one that you are wearing. In this case, as soon as you can, you must immerse your crystal for several seconds in a solution of salted water to purify it.

The quartz crystal is one of the most perfect physical forms in the universe and this perfection makes it very useful on a therapeutic level. It acts like a catalyst of our own perfection, because deep down we are all perfect. Our being is of light and emanates directly from the divine world.

At birth, we have all the potential necessary for accomplishing everything we want. The negative situations which we experience throughout our lives create imperfections in us, but I repeat that the essence of our being is perfect. It is this perfection which is called on to reverberate in the presence of the quartz crystal which itself reflects perfection. This is called the 'law of harmony'.

For example, if you press down on the pedal of a piano to raise the pads that press against the strings and then you hit middle C, all the other C strings will start to vibrate. This is the phenomenon of resonance. All the C notes will resound on the same frequency as the note you have hit, without you having to touch them.

The same thing happens between ourselves and the crystal. When we are in the presence of a quartz crystal, which is pure light and which vibrates on the pitch of perfection, we ourselves join in the vibration thanks to the perfection that exists inside ourselves. This perfection, which is our very being, will be amplified and will manifest itself through better health, a greater equilibrium and the realisation of our potential.

In our society, which has a tendency to stereotype and pigeon-hole, we must constantly focus on achieving our full potential. The quartz crystal will help us achieve this.

Faults or cracks within certain crystals create the appearance of rainbows. The prism of colours apparent inside the crystal increases its potential for amplification. All quartz crystals amplify intentions and thought-forms, but those which contain rainbows do so to an even greater degree.

Clear quartz crystals heal tears and imbalances in your

electromagnetic field. Heavy smoking or drinking, traumatic shock, overwork, etc. can all cause holes or tears in your electromagnetic field.

I have seen people with electromagnetic fields that were denser in some places and thinner in others. Such people generally feel very ill at ease and unbalanced. The quartz crystal can help to heal up and balance the electromagnetic field.

The clear quartz crystal also has the ability to refresh and calm the 'kundalini' when it has been prematurely awoken. The kundalini, which is also called 'the serpent's fire', is a very special energy coiled up at the base of the spine. This energy lies dormant in most of us – and fortunately so, since when it is woken up it immediately looks for a way to flow up the spine until it reaches the head.

A good image of the kundalini can be found in Egyptian hieroglyphics. The image of a pharaoh with a cobra on the forehead, situated in the position of the 'third eye' signifies that the pharaoh has succeeded in getting the kundalini to climb up to the third eye and display itself as a clairvoyant.

However, when the kundalini is woken up before the chakras (the centres of energy found along the spine) are all open, it will climb up until it reaches one that is closed and will stay there blocked. The energy will remain there too and display itself specifically through this centre.

The majority of people whose kundalini is awoken prematurely will present an unbridled sexuality, with their 'serpent's fire' checked in the second centre. They will also sometimes display problems of digestion, procreation, assimilation and elimination.

Today there are plenty of spiritual schools that work with this energy and attempt to awaken it. However, they sometimes make the mistake of not having effected, as a preliminary, the work of clarification and purification around the central channel and different centres of energy. As a result, the flow of kundalini energy is restricted and unstable. With the quartz crystal it is possible to appease and re-balance this force of the kundalini.

It can happen that a clear quartz crystal has a key which is not in harmony with your own basic key, since all of us vibrate at a certain precise frequency.

The best way of finding your basic key is to sing the first note that comes to you when you wake up in the morning and to remember it. Repeat this experiment for several weeks. You will find that a particular note recurs persistently. This is your fundamental key.

Each quartz crystal also sings in a fundamental key. When she was young, Dhyani Ywahoo had to find a crystal that had been buried in the woods as part of her training. To find it, she followed the sound that each crystal gave off. You too can learn later how to hear crystals singing, because all crystals sing and it is possible to hear the sound of each one of them.

As I have already mentioned, it can happen that your basic key and that of the crystal strike a dissonant chord. For example, if you vibrate on the note C and your quartz crystal vibrates on F sharp, the chord is not very harmonious. This dissonance between you and the crystal will cause nausea and dizziness, you will feel bad in yourself and so on. In brief, you will suffer disagreeable and undesirable effects.

You should not, however, believe that the crystal is essentially bad. There is quite simply an incompatibility. In such a case, you can pass the crystal on to someone else who is in harmony with it or put the crystal to another use where you will no longer be physically in its presence.

Clear quartz is the crystal most adaptable to the human being. We all possess an etheric field, the first energy field around our body. This field has a hexagonal molecular structure. That is to say, each molecule of this energy body has six sides. The quartz crystal's electromagnetic field and its molecules are also hexagonal. For this reason it is well adapted for the human body and it is no coincidence that the clear quartz crystal is the one most frequently found on the planet surface. About 65 per cent of the substance that makes up the Earth is silica.

You should never pass a coloured crystal through someone else's electromagnetic field as such a gesture can be very harmful for them. Only clear quartz crystals can be passed right through another individual's electromagnetic field. We call this a crystal bath since it cleans the field of positive ions. Certain other crystals can be used locally at precise points of the body. However, it is only with the clear quartz crystal that you can work, in complete safety, right through the field.

When the clear quartz crystal is as large as two fists, it is called a generator. It is too big to be used in healing, but it should be able to work in guarding thought-forms or amplifying particular intentions.

AMETHYST

Let us now look at the properties of the amethyst crystal, which is the stone of transformation. It is associated with Venus and the number three. It is the stone of travel and, because of that, it is good to have one in the car. A number of people have told me that the amethyst in their car has saved their lives. I travel a lot and drive quickly and not very carefully. I have never had an accident since I started keeping an amethyst in the boot.

The amethyst is sometimes known as the 'flame of transmutation'. In fact, this stone is a quartz with magnesium inclusions, which give it its violet colour. When a crystal does not have any inclusions, the organised structure of its molecules allows you to see through it. The crystal is clear and translucent. On the other hand, when a crystal has inclusions spread across its molecules, as is the case with the amethyst, it will often have a colour particular to itself. This becomes important when you want to work with the vibration associated with the colour.

Basically all pure crystals are clear. For example, there are certain ones, called beryls, which are completely transparent but when they have inclusions that colour them green, they are called emeralds and when they have inclusions that colour them blue, they are called aquamarines. Thus the type of crystal varies according to the colour.

In the case of amethyst, there are magnesium inclusions which create an ultraviolet spectrum, symbolising alchemic processes on both a physical and spiritual level. This stone can, therefore, be used to change the bad habits of alcoholism, drugs or other excess of any kind.

In such a case, you place a little piece of polished amethyst under the tongue of the person displaying these symptoms. There are glands lodged under the tongue which communicate with the whole biochemical system of the human body. The little piece of amethyst reacts with these glands and transforms the impulse to consume the given substance.

In our society, people are continually being pressured into becoming part of pre-established patterns, into responding to stereotypes and into becoming cogs in the wheel of the 'ideal' society. Because of this, we are not always able to express our potential. When this energy mounts inside us, because it runs contrary to the patterns established by society, we sometimes channel it into activities that reduce the vitality of our bodies on both the physical and spiritual levels.

Overeating, drinking too much, gambling (where one invariably loses), compulsive smoking and so on are all activities which reduce physical and spiritual vitality. In the end, we become dependent on them. Over a period of time, the body gets used to this way of behaving and looks for it automatically. It is here that habits set in.

To help change these habits, we can work directly on a biochemical level by putting the little piece of amethyst under the tongue. The body will thus receive a message ordering it to change and will take the mounting energy, accept it and channel it elsewhere. Moreover, it is difficult to drink, smoke or eat with a stone in one's mouth!

You should normally keep the piece of amethyst in your mouth for about ten minutes, the time necessary to change the urge and direct it elsewhere. You can, for example, re-orientate this energy and put it into playing music or another activity that you enjoy doing. This energy is not in itself bad, rather it is the habit we have adopted of directing it in such a destructive way, that is an obstacle to the realisation of our full potential.

Alcoholism, drug addiction and other dependencies represent an illness of the soul, whose progression can be stopped by a spiritual programme of reorientation and rehabilitation. The technique recommended with the amethyst will not replace the work carried out by recognised and qualified groups or associations. However, it can help restore a balance and change the programming that dependence has instilled into the body.

Here is one case of a woman who cured her alcoholic husband in this way.

Since the man was too far advanced in his addiction simply to use a small piece of amethyst under his tongue – he was drinking almost two litres of whisky a day – she programmed an amethyst crystal which she put inside a bottle. He drank all the whisky without noticing the amethyst. She then took the crystal out of the bottle, purified and programmed it again and put it back in another bottle. She continued doing this for several days.

Then she noticed that her husband had replaced the

whisky with wine. This time she put the piece of amethyst in with the wine, taking care to purify and reprogramme the crystal for each bottle. After that he went on to beer and she continued with the same treatment. Finally the husband registered with Alcoholics Anonymous and underwent treatment. He stopped drinking. It was only some years later that he found out what his wife had been doing.

This example illustrates clearly how the amethyst can work and how one can use it to alter bad habits and addictions.

Amethyst has a light refraction index of 2.55, greater than that of clear quartz, and can be used as a crystal of protection, since it repels more than it attracts. If you need plenty of protection, it is even better to use amethyst than clear quartz. (Pink quartz can be used for very emotional people, but it is important that it is translucent.) Just as with the quartz, you should wear an amethyst next to the spiritual plexus and purify it every day when using it for protection. It will appease the lower chakras and boost the energy of the upper ones.

You can also use amethyst for sexual differentiation.

Certain people have difficulty in determining or understanding their sexual orientation. It is important that they discover who they really are, since if such people are not able to understand and follow their orientation they will be unhappy all their life.

I knew a woman, a pupil of Oh Shinnah, who was married and had had children. She had been unhappy all her life, until she met Oh Shinnah, who suggested that she meditate with an amethyst. As a result, she found that her sexual orientation was quite different from what she had assumed and, thanks to the amethyst, it now became clear to her. She divorced and re-established her life in the company of other women. Today she is an extraordinary healer and would never have realised this had she not understood who she really was.

The important thing is not so much the choice that you make but rather to understand properly who you are on a sexual level. The amethyst will help you reach this point and, in order to do so, you must meditate with it.

You must be careful when working with an amethyst. It can have adverse effects for people who are hyperactive, autistic, schizophrenic, retarded or single-minded. (In the last case, I mean this as someone who has narrow views or a closed mind. For example, a businessman who refuses to see anything outside his vision of a materialistic world.) In such cases, the amethyst cannot help. It will clash with the person and quite often throw them off balance.

Sometimes you can use the amethyst to help you perfect the results of your work – for example, when you have made some perceptible progress with a client and need to complete the business.

This stone is the most powerful of the transformers and with some people it is necessary to proceed with caution. Often it would be better to work with another stone.

CITRINE

Let us now consider the citrine and analyse its properties so that we can learn how to use it correctly.

First we must distinguish between two types of citrine: madeira and golden. The first is orange-brown in colour and the second yellow. The madeira citrine has an orange streak and the golden citrine a yellow one. The two stones are both quartz but with particular inclusions.

The citrine is also called the coyote stone. According to American Indian mythology, the coyote is the one who plays tricks, obliging others to learn despite their bitter resistance. Therefore the citrine is used for those who are most resistant to treatment, as well as for the narrow-minded and those with fixed ideas.

When in contact with the citrine one has a tendency to open oneself to the upper vibrations, to the spiritual realities that one has not been in the habit of recognising. For the businessman struggling with his fixed ideas, I suggest offering him a tie-pin containing a citrine, which he can wear every day. You do not have to tell him why. Your intention, which will be amplified by the crystal, will be enough to bring about a change. In doing this, you will have played a little 'coyote trick' on him.

This stone stimulates both the mental and spiritual body and eliminates the toxins in the lower chakras. It helps open our minds to superior ideas on a spiritual level. What is more, it thins out the energy field where this has become too dense. You can sometimes see, for example, darkish areas in the atmosphere around a particular person, reflecting the trau-matic relationship that person has with themself or some trauma that has affected their life which continues to live in their electromagnetic field. The citrine will disperse this congestion.

The majority of illnesses described as psychosomatic display these symptoms. Asthma is a good example of such an illness and reacts well to the use of citrine.

When you are able to work with the citrine crystal, you should always start the treatment with a madeira citrine. Once the work is well underway, you can move on to the golden citrine.

The citrine is also used in the treatment of traumas. Take the case of a man who is involved in a car accident and who witnesses the death of his wife and child. It is absolutely essential to enter into contact with the suffering and all that he has lost. He has to feel it and express it. The shock is sometimes so terrible that any expression is blocked up inside. The experience is repressed, buried in the depths of his conscience, because it is just too painful. In such a case, there is no reaction whatsoever and the man keeps the sadness unseen and unexpressed in his energy field, to be released later at some inopportune moment.

It is imperative that the affected person is able to cry, to express what they feel. If not, the pain will accumulate, without any purification, and that will prove very harmful. The ideal thing to do is to hold a piece of citrine in the hand. You can help, too, by visualising the light of the citrine and emitting it.

So, in all cases of serious trauma, the citrine is the first stone to use.

HERKIMER

The herkimer (milky quartz), which also belongs to the quartz family, is a crystal with two points directly opposite one another at an angle of 180 degrees. However, unlike other quartz crystals with two points, the herkimer is slightly thicker and harder. Generally quartz has a hardness of 7, while the herkimer can be measured at 7.5.

This is the stone of dreams, of astral travel and excursions outside one's body. It is used, for example, by those who want to make it easier to escape their body and reintegrate it and by those who want to remember their dreams.

To start with, the herkimer will send us, in a dream world, to the antipodes of our normal habits. It particularly likes transition, so we can use it in pregnancy or to help in the passing on of the dead. It is not a stone to be worn or to be carried around (in the car, for example) and absolutely no jewellery made with this stone should be worn except in bed. It is possible to overdose on a herkimer tincture, so be careful!

SMOKY QUARTZ

The antidote to the herkimer is the smoky quartz, which will bring back to reality anyone who has misused the power of the herkimer.

There is one thing you should watch out for when choosing a smoky quartz. You must not confuse it with a clear quartz that has been irradiated and become completely black. The effect of such a stone and that of a true smoky quartz will not be the same. It should be light to dark brown in colour, to be effective.

Smoky quartz will help people regain contact with reality and assist them in achieving a more solid and down-to-earth existence. Those who always have a tendency to plan great projects, who talk a lot about them but realise little, who live in their dreams or who are always undecided when faced with a choice of situations are those who will benefit most from using smoky quartz.

It is important that our life and our spirituality are both solid. It is not for nothing that we have a physical body. We must live in it, be ourselves as human beings and accept the reality of things. Smoky quartz will help us display this more practical, down-to-earth and solid spirit.

CHRYSOPRASE

Chrysoprase is a light green stone, often with colour irregularities within the stone. It works on the optic nerve (by looking at the stone) to stimulate the brain in order to regain contact with reality. It is suitable for treating cases of neurosis, psychosis, schizophrenia, etc.

PERIDOT

The peridot is a lime-coloured crystal presenting two streaks – green and yellow. It is one of the rare stones to carry two colours simultaneously. When mounted on a piece of golden jewellery, it provides powerful protection against bad forces.

You can use the peridot to counteract influenza, depression, obesity, constipation, ulcers, diabetes, prostate problems, fear and nightmares, for which it is particularly effective. You can either attach the stone to the bed or to your clothes, where it will change or remove the context of the nightmare.

AQUAMARINE

This light blue crystal is also used in the fight of good forces against evil. One can use it, for example, in the case of exorcism. It incites one to tell the truth and is very effective for reconciliation and human relations in general.

The human being is certainly much stronger than any bad entity because the human possesses a body, which a spirit does not have. It is, moreover, the reason why evil, negative and disincarnate spirits search out people in order to possess them, since they want to re-embody themselves. Because we have something that the bad spirits have not (our bodies), we are stronger from the outset.

On the other hand, the evil spirit does have a way in, a means of influencing human beings: fear. It is this which feeds the spirits and gives them their strength. If you have absolutely no fear of the forces of evil, then they can have no influence over you.

There are two natural fears: that of falling and that of sudden noise. All other fears are creations of your imagination. You do not need them and they can even harm you and slow down your evolution. Fear attracts that which you are afraid of. If you are afraid of thieves, they will come. If you fear fire, you will be a victim of it. If you are frightened of the devil, he will show himself in you.

You can confront fear, because it is very cowardly. All the time that you run away from it, it will follow you like your shadow. The moment that you turn and face it, it will be the one to run away. The only way to get rid of fear is to tackle it head on, to analyse it, to find out where it comes from and why it is there.

One day a sales representative came to consult me. He had had an accident on a bridge and, ever since, he was unable to cross it. Each time he went to drive over it, fear took hold of him and he froze on the spot. He had to get out and have his car towed over it or ask his wife to come and drive it. Since she had to call a taxi to come and meet him, this was not very practical.

I advised him to walk on to the bridge and go as far as he felt he was able to. Then, where he had stopped, he should spend some time thinking about the accident and let out his emotions and feelings. He followed my advice and did this for seven days. Now he crosses the bridge in his car without any problem.

A woman also came to consult me about her problem of fear, but this time it was spiders. The slightest thought that there might be spiders in the house and she felt ill. Whenever she saw one, she got in a terrible state.

As treatment I put the woman completely alone in a dark room. Then I made her visualise a small spider in the corner. By the end of therapy, she was able to visualise lots of large hairy black tarantulas climbing all over her body. Now, she has absolutely no fear of spiders and can even pick them up in her hand.

With just these two examples, it is easy to see how, in confronting your fear, you can reduce and even eliminate it.

The reason why aquamarine is so effective in exorcism is that it encourages one to tell the truth. When a person, for whatever reason, has chosen to welcome a spirit inside which aggravates them and prevents them from being their true self, the therapist can use the force of truth to help that person rid themselves of the evil spirit.

Knowing the name of the spirit is useful. With an aquamarine, the exorcist can confront it and force it to reveal who it is. The spirit will have to give its name, because it will have to tell the truth. It can, of course, remain silent. In this case, the exorcist will say to it: 'You, who will not tell me your name, go away'. This means of addressing the spirit will force it to leave the person it is inhabiting, because the power of the voice and that of the body – if one does not feel any fear – are stronger that any evil being. As Jesus said in the Bible: 'Get thee behind me, Satan'.

Oh Shinnah told me another very interesting story. When the Allies defeated the Germans at the end of the Second World War, they entered one concentration camp where a large number of Jews had been confined in huts. Curiously, the German guards were as thin, ill and badly dressed as the majority of Jews in the camp, with the exception of one hut. Here the prisoners were not so thin, in better health and better dressed than all the others.

In this particular hut there was a large wooden chest, inside which was a kind of monster made of earth and stone representing the human form. The American Indians call this a 'wendigo'. For the Jews who know the Cabbala, this is known as a 'golem'. To help counteract their fear, the people in this hut had succeeded in breathing life into this figure and, since it was made of earth and stone, it could not be killed like a mortal. With the help of this monster to which they had given life, the Jews had managed to survive better than the others, intimidating everyone with the power of this 'golem'.

It is only fear that can expose one to evil forces but this is why they are so powerful in our actual world, since our society functions a great deal on fear and uses it like a teaching instrument. Our system of education is based on the principle of reward and punishment: 'If you commit a crime, you will be punished. And if you have not done your homework correctly, you will get bad marks and your parents will be angry.'

From the earliest age we are taught to respond to fear more than love. As a result, we have created a very critical situation in the world. People are afraid, react to that fear and work with it. They are afraid that someone else has a larger gun or a bigger bomb than they have which threatens their health, their well-being or their economy. They are afraid that there will be nothing more to eat or nothing more to wear, so they strive to accumulate material possessions. The result is a society totally dependent on the consumption of goods, a system which itself impoverishes the developing nations. This in turn creates a civilisation where certain people have plenty and others have nothing at all. Fear encourages this way of life.

As therapists, we must be very conscious of the existence of fear. We must be ready to confront it and not to let it set in.

CHRYSOCOLL, MALACHITE AND TURQUOISE

These stones, which are turquoise to dark green in colour, help in diluting fear, when it takes a grip around the solar plexus, and can make it disappear altogether. They are also effective around the spleen and the pancreas and work well in maintaining balance.

Malachite communicates its forces very well through direct contact with the skin, better in fact than most other stones. One notices this straight away just by touching it.

For its part, chrysocoll has currently replaced turquoise in terms of usefulness. As with all living things, stones are in the process of evolution. Equally, some are degenerating and the turquoise is one of them. This means it no longer has the same power as it used to have.

Turquoise symbolises spirituality, the sky, the Heavenly Father. In days gone by, it was highly regarded as a spiritual stone which put mankind in touch with the divine and holy reality, which inspired human beings and which put clarity into their thoughts.

Today chrysocoll tends to take the place of turquoise. Its evolution is very quick. Some years ago its hardness was 3 or 4 or sometimes 5, which meant that it was not really hard enough for making jewellery. Nowadays you can find it, alloyed with quartz, with a much greater hardness of 6 or 7 and a beautiful deep blue-green colour.

What is more, turquoise is not strictly a crystal, since its molecules are not arranged in a geometric form. Its structure is more amorphous than that of chrysocoll.

You can use chrysocoll for dispersing fears around the solar plexus, thanks to its spiritual element which helps you abandon your fear and replace it with love.

Old pieces of jewellery using turquoise will have retained all their power and will have kept the spiritual vibration of the element sky. Turquoise will also ensure protection when it is given by a friend.

Chrysocoll and malachite are the two main stones used to dispel fear or prevent it from affecting you. Above all, you must not react by letting yourself give any ground to fear. When you see fear coming , you must simply say to yourself: 'I am not afraid of it. I will leave it to follow its own course. It does not belong inside me'.

If a particular fear persists, analyse it and try to find out why it is there. For example, if you are afraid of water, go to meet it at the bank of a stream or lake and stay there. The images that are stirred up inside you and your feelings at that moment will help you to know why that fear is there. When you know that, it will go away of its own accord.

ROCK CRYSTAL

I now want to discuss another type of stone called rock crystal, which is a quartz crystal, but colourless. It is mainly used for costume jewellery. Sometimes it is used for pendulums and it is very pretty hanging in front of a window where it releases its rainbow reflections.

It is however, not used in American Indian crystal healing.

DIOPTASE

Dioptase is emerald green and grows on surfaces as short clusters of crystal. This is useful for treating high blood pressure and Parkinson's disease.

GARNET

Garnet is a very deep red stone and, as with all stones belonging to the red ray, it is energising. Less powerful and softer than a ruby, it can often initiate stimulation of the body, and can then be followed by the ruby with its greater power. It is used for the whole of the endocrine system and for blood diseases (particularly, in this latter case, in the form of tinctures).

This is a stone of mystery, because it enables one to work on what is sometimes known as 'the time between', that is to say the time between dimensions, at dawn just before the sun rises or at nightfall, just after it has set. It is a very particular time, when the crack between the worlds is open. Different types of magician practise at this time and the garnet helps their work.

It has a peculiarity among all the other stones in that it is almost inactive if it has not been cut and polished. In order to liberate the colour which it keeps hidden, and to gain the maximum influence from it on a therapeutic level, the garnet must be cut and polished.

RUBY

The ruby is a brighter red and has instantaneous energy. It will work on all degenerative diseases by rebuilding, re-energising, fortifying and stimulating. A type of corundum, this stone is very powerful and will enable you to disperse any negative emotions that have crystallised in the blood system.

The ruby also symbolises love, but that of a Christian kind, unconditional love, of one who gives their life for those they love – as Jesus did on the Cross. It is no coincidence that the Pope wears a ruby, because it is the symbol of love and of the true sacrifice of the ego for service to others.

Sometimes the ruby has a tendency to provoke quite a resounding karma in egoists and very self-centred people. In effect, the ruby can amplify the change in the karma of such people, since they are working against this stone's energy. In order to wear a ruby, it is necessary to have an altruistic conscience and be generous.

When using a tincture of ruby or garnet, you must afterwards restore the equilibrium by means of a green or blue stone. For example, in the case of a person suffering from anaemia, a tincture of ruby can be used for a month, but must then be followed for one week with a tincture of emerald or aquamarine to mollify the force of the ruby.

Tinctures of ruby and garnet are very powerful and can result in an overdose. Therefore you must be careful not to overstep the limits of the system's reserves. You must not forget that the vibration of these tinctures invokes the energy in your system and sets it in motion. If you abuse it, you can burn yourself.

PYRITES (IRON)

Also called 'fool's gold', this is never worn in jewellery, but its symmetrical beauty is pleasing to the eye. It can be a useful support (visualising) for fortifying the blood in cases of anaemia or iron deficiency and it helps good management of possessions one already owns.

TOPAZ

When I talk about topaz, I am referring to the golden yellow kind. (There are also other types such as blue and smoked topaz.)

This stone is the symbol of the sun god and of Sagittarius and it is beneficial for the eyes, the nervous system and the intellect in general. It stimulates creative energies and is therefore particularly favourable for artists and the elaboration of projects. It is also called the stone of invisibility, because it allows one to pass unnoticed when held in the left hand.

Here is an interesting anecdote that illustrates the stone's qualities.

A resistance movement had been organised by several tribes of American Indians near Wounded Knee to contest and assert their rights. The place was particularly symbolic for them, since it was here that some soldiers had already massacred many of their women, children and old folk. The army and militia surrounded the spot where the American Indians had gathered. Oh Shinnah was asked to go and find some warriors to help them, but all the routes leading out of the place were blocked. It was then that an old sage gave her a topaz, telling her to hold it in her left hand while singing a song that he taught her. They then left to find the warriors.

When they reached the police blockade, they switched off the lights of the car and Oh Shinnah started singing the song that she had just learned. The policemen did not even turn round, since they had seen nothing, and Oh Shinnah was able to pass through without any problem. She did the same on her way back.

Here is another story.

One of Oh Shinnah's students wanted to experiment with the powers of the topaz. Holding a stone in her left hand, she joined the queue in a 'fast food' restaurant. But no one paid any attention to her. The waitress spoke to the people either side and to those in front and behind, but ignored her completely. It was only when she wrapped the topaz in some red fabric that the waitress realised she was there.

So, if you want to pass unnoticed, I suggest that you try this out for yourself.

The topaz has another interesting particularity. If it is given in the form of jewellery by a loved one and it changes colour, this is a sign that the person is not faithful.

SAPPHIRE

Let us now consider the sapphire. Bearing in mind that there are several types, I will concentrate here just on the very deep blue sapphire – the indigo. Sometimes you can find it almost blue-black.

This stone, which provides access to some very deep levels of the mind, brings on sleep and can stimulate very intense states of devotion. It also enhances prayer. This is the reason why oracles and sorcerers used to use the sapphire in days gone by, since it enabled them to develop particularly deep levels of perception and they were thus better able to respond to those who came to consult them.

Sapphire essence is used to counteract deteriorating vision and general problems of sight when applied as eye-drops. It can also be used for sterilising containers, but the water must first be distilled. The sapphire's vibration is also very beneficial for problems with the ears, nose, throat and lungs.

AZURITE

Azurite is a deep-blue crystal which grows embedded and encrusting in clusters. It very useful for curing tendon trouble. To do this, you must place the stone in the etheric electro-magnetic field near the affected spot. Swing the stone, in a movement that follows the length of the bone, for a few minutes. To start with, use this treatment every half-hour, then every hour and afterwards two or three times a day until the effect is felt and the problem disappears completely. You can repeat this as often as is necessary. It is quite spectacular, producing results very quickly.

Azurite is also used in the same way for all instances of back pain and other muscular problems. In most cases you will notice a reduction in the pain and the inflammation, leading to the cure of the affected area.

Never attempt to prepare an essence from this stone since it gives off sulphur when mixed with water.

RED CORAL

Red coral is not a crystal. It belongs at the same time to the animal, vegetable and mineral kingdoms and, for the American Indians, it symbolises fundamental strength. As such, it is used in the restructuring and growth of the bone cells.

Just as you do with azurite, you place a piece of red coral in the electromagnetic field near the affected spot. In fact, this stone is often used in conjunction with azurite. You begin with red coral to revitalise the bone cells and then use azurite to relieve the pain. This way, the cure will be a lot quicker.

In the case of a fracture, red coral will stimulate the growth of the cells and accelerate recovery. Here is an example:

One of my aunts, who was 75 years old, broke a bone in her foot. At this age, the healing process is necessarily much slower. I advised her to apply a treatment of azurite and red coral. When she next saw her doctor, three weeks after the accident, he was very surprised to see that the bone had reset completely and the fracture had disappeared.

Red coral is also very useful in treating cases of bone cancer.

ROSE QUARTZ

This stone is a smoky pink coloured quartz. It is associated with the chakra and the ray of the heart and is therefore prescribed for all heart problems, whether physical or emotional. It soothes, calms and relaxes the person who uses it.

It is therefore of great help to hyperactive children or babies who cry a lot. Give them a piece of rose quartz large enough so that there is no danger of it being swallowed. They will calm down almost immediately.

Rose quartz is a micro-crystalline stone, which is why one normally finds it cut. The crystal exists, but it is very small and very rare.

AMAZONITE

This is a soft, clear green micro-crystalline stone. It is excellent for reducing and eliminating stress and for calming the nervous system.

MOONSTONE

The moonstone, which is soft and translucent with a yellow to blue-white sheen, is very popular among women, helps in harmonising the monthly cycle by regularising and easing the pains. It also stimulates fertility. This stone represents the great Mother Goddess and is therefore tuned to lunar energy.

For women who suffer from premenstrual and menstrual pains, a tincture of moonstone taken three or four days before the periods start will help considerably. For anyone, man or woman, this stone can help in tuning in to female energy. As such, it is of benefit in treating machos and misogynists alike.

According to the American Indian tradition, understanding the female cycle brings with it great wisdom. You should first understand that all women are superior to men because their cycle, a *natural* cycle inscribed into their biological code, made them what they are. It is an initiation in itself and gives them the potential to communicate with the force of the divine Holy Mother, who produces all life in the universe. When a woman is 'in her moon' (having her period), this force runs through her and makes her stronger. The American Indian believes this is the greatest 'medicine' that exists. If properly respected, this power becomes a resource.

In days gone by, when a woman was in her moon, she withdrew into the moon's shelter. She did not work, she did not prepare any meals, she did not mix with others in the community and she retired to a spot out of the way where all those women who were having their periods went to meditate, pray and carry out certain ceremonies. The very old and wise women, as well as certain men who were known as the 'impulsive dreamers', came to meet and teach them. The 'impulsive dreamer' was the only man allowed, because he had a very developed female energy. During this time, the women learned to accept and live with their femininity, which contributed to their flowering as women.

For the American Indians, the woman's superiority rests in the fact that the men do not have this particular cycle, this monthly initiation. In addition, when girls have their first period, they always celebrate the fact. It is like the promise of a new life for the community. In certain cases, the celebrations can last for three whole days.

Among the Tenehs (Apaches), the girl traditionally had to keep her arms stretched out for 24 hours. To help herself do this, she would eat certain plants. Sometimes people would come from afar just to touch her, since she embodied the Holy Mother Goddess in all her purity. As the men had no similar, natural initiation into adulthood, they invented their own initiation rituals to enable them to become men.

For example, they would climb a mountain and stay there for several days, sometimes as many as nine, without eating, drinking or sleeping. In this way they put themselves on the same level as the spiritual kingdom, where one has no need of food, water or sleep, and learned from the Spirit their role and mission on Earth and their power as a human being. In this atmosphere of solitude and the darkness of night, they faced their internal devils and learned about the courage, mastery and control that leads to maturity. In short, they became men.

While such a visionary quest used to exist for men and enabled them to acquire such maturity, today these rites have been completely forgotten or changed. It is because of this that you will often hear women complaining about their husbands' immaturity. Plenty of men behave like children. They have not reached this level of maturity that women acquire naturally.

One must also see sexuality as something quite natural. Its expression is part of life and it must be lived naturally as a thing of beauty. Sexuality is everywhere: in atoms, stones, among plants and animals. It is an integral part of life. The precepts of our society, which make it something shameful, bad or evil, are the cause of all the problems that are linked with it today. Sexually transmitted diseases, sexual deviations, violence, rape, abuse and AIDS, for example, all emanate to a great extent from the misconception that sex is bad when not exercised within marriage or certain other cultural contexts. There is nothing more natural or more normal than sex.

When a woman is in her moon, she is stronger than other men and women and can, during this time, sap the energy of others without even realising it. Being stronger, she attracts the vital force from other people. It is one of the reasons that explains why, years ago, women left their group when they began a period so as not to harm the others. I never sleep with my wife during her moon so that I will not wake up tired the next morning.

Equally, it is very important that women do not treat or perform therapy on anyone during their monthly cycle, since they can, without wishing to, deprive that person of their energy. If it happens that you have to do this all the same, put a piece of moonstone in your navel and keep it there throughout the time of the treatment. Do not forget to remove it as soon as you have finished.

You can sometimes hear a little hissing noise when you remove the moonstone. This indicates that the energy is starting to circulate again, since the stone has the property of containing your energy and preventing you from absorbing that of the patient during the treatment.

When Oh Shinnah was younger, she never went to work during her periods and made this a condition of her employment. If her employers did not accept this, then she changed her job. In this way she asserted herself and demanded respect for the female force manifesting itself in her.

In western societies, the woman has for a long time been considered inferior and she is still considered to be so. In the autochthonous societies, however, she is regarded as equal to men, who learn to respect her and develop their own 'female' qualities such as listening, tolerating and welcoming. There is a great strength in gentleness. Men too can cry; it is neither shameful nor a sign of weakness. In fact, sometimes it requires real courage to reveal one's emotions in front of others. Those who never cry accumulate forces which, in the long term, make them violent and indifferent to others. One only has to look at all the violence that exists in today's society, which teaches that a man should never cry, to see the truth in that.

For a man who is narrow-minded or macho, you can use the moonstone to help him open up and make contact with his female qualities. At the same time, you might be able to rediscover the rites of passage that have been created for men and encourage him to perform them. He will then become more mature and not feel so threatened by women or by the expression of emotions.

TOURMALINE
(of the green variety)

This harmonises, balances and soothes. It is efficient against heart and circulation problems. It dissolves blood clots and can be used to treat both low and high blood pressure.

TOURMALINE
(water melon)

This helps balance the lunar and solar forces in the body (yin and yang). It enables the physical body to adapt to radiation and eliminate excessive radioactivity.

EMERALD

Like all the other green stones, the emerald has an effect on equilibrium. It strengthens the heart and the blood system and helps one's harmony and communication with the devas (some of the good spirits of Hindu mythology). It is excellent for providing a balance, notably after using a ruby or garnet.

The emerald will inspire and fill you with a feeling of equanimity. It will regenerate tired nerves and balance the level of glucose in the blood.

AMBER

This is not actually a crystal, but a fossil, however it helps to remove the pain young children suffer when growing teeth. It balances the yin and yang (masculine and feminine) forces and encourages imagination and the recall of interior landscapes.

CARNELIAN

The carnelian, which belongs to the orange ray, is a form of agate. You use it for regulating problems of communication, expression and even speech. It is also useful for clearing the mind and can improve your concentration.

Unlike other stones, which do not need to be used close to the affected spot, carnelian must be worn very near the area you want to treat – for example, near the throat when working with problems of expression or communication.

It will also recharge and correct imbalances in the etheric body, and the frequencies cornelian emits are beneficial in counteracting energy deficiency.

AGATE

The agates come in a variety of colours and display different lines or layers, symbolising the integration of different facets of the body. When you go into deep meditation you will become aware of the body's complexity, because that is precisely what meditation aims to do: integrate the different facets of the body in order to arrive at a united, balanced whole.

The agate is very beneficial for this process, which is why it is also a good protecting stone when travelling. Having to uproot oneself can create a feeling of instability and of being lost. This stone will help you become more settled, wherever you happen to be. It is why I always have an agate hanging from the rear-view mirror of my car.

It should be noted that there is a lot of quartz in agates.

JADE

As for jade, this stone symbolises serenity and meditation. It has an incredible hardness and it is commonly associated with oriental spirituality. Black jade will assimilate and contain negativity, thus assuming a protective role.

The true jadeite (the hardest type of jade) comes in a range of colours: all shades of green from clear to olive and dark green, clear brown, opalescent, milky white, yellow, etc. However, what is often sold on the market and called jade is in fact nephrite, which ranges in colour from pale to dark green and does not have the same properties as jade. The price will always give you a good indication of what the stone really is. Jadeite is very expensive, while nephrite costs much less.

Jade will help any work with the dying, thanks to its qualities of eternity, so if you have to treat people in palliative care, it is helpful to wear a jadeite.

JASPER (GREEN)

Jasper helps to re-establish lost contact with nature and the Earth. It generates feelings of unity with life and is useful against nausea.

DIAMOND

I will now look at the most precious stone – diamond. Of cubic geometric form, this is the most perfect of all the stones and one that has reached the summit of its evolution. It symbolises the Unique One, the Father who gives birth to all and in particular to will and fidelity.

Unlike other stones which are made up of at least two elements, the diamond contains just one – carbon. It is the hardest of all the stones. In the scale of hardness, only the diamond achieves the highest rating, that of 10. Its cubic construction displays a very balanced physical organisation. In a clear diamond we can see all the colours of the rainbow, just as there are diamonds of all colours.

Because the diamond is a powerful amplifier, you must be careful when you wear it, since it will increase everything without discrimination. If you are in good health, it will enhance it. On the other hand, if you are not well, it will aggravate your illness. If you have negative thoughts or emotions, this crystal will amplify them and the karma that comes to you will be strong and rapid. You will learn very quickly by experience, but this can be disagreeable.

You may have noticed that, in general, women refrain from wearing their diamonds all the time. They will wear their wedding ring constantly, but only wear other diamonds on special occasions. This is very sensible because, on such occasions, we feel happier and this sentiment will be amplified by the diamonds we wear. On the other hand, in our daily life we go through a whole range of emotions which are not always happy, and which could also be amplified by the diamond. In these circumstances, it is preferable not to wear one.

PEARL

The most feminine stone that exists is the pearl and it is rare to see men wearing them.

The pearl corresponds to the energy of the moon and of water and provides effective protection against the forces of perversion which can be unleashed by certain men. Pearls will attract these bad forces and stop them from getting lodged in a woman's electromagnetic field.

Unlike all other stones, to purify pearls you should pass them through salted water. You can do this by putting one hand in the water and letting the necklace run between your fingers as you pull it with the other hand. Salt-water pearls do not initially need to be purified for a whole week, since they come from the sea.

OPAL

The predominant element of opal is water (as with the pearl). Do not use fire opal when you want to work with the blue ray. It is used for amplifying the feminine nature of a being.

OBSIDIAN

The obsidian is a glittering black stone which, when polished, takes on the appearance of black glass. It comes from volcanic lava that has solidified very rapidly.

It is a very inert stone, which has not had time to crystallise. Therefore it is not really a crystal. It is very shiny and has often been used as a divinatory mirror, with which people have tried to see the future or work with clairvoyance. The state of rest and emptiness provoked by this stone enhances such work.

LABRADORITE

This stone contains grey-green, blue and white; it also contains its fair share of unknowns and mysteries. We do know that it helps access to some levels of more subtle clairvoyance, and the physical world. It can create illusions when the research is motivated by dubious intentions. One must remain vigilant when working with this stone.

BLOODSTONE

This is a micro-crystalline stone, dark green in colour with blood red points. It is used to strangle haemorrhages and for cleansing the blood of poisons or pain. To do this, it is sufficient just to apply the stone directly to the affected part of the body.

Bloodstone is also sometimes useful for treating liver complaints.

CELESTITE

A colourless to white or bluish tinted crystal, effective for treating migraines and headaches. Its tincture is calming and soothing in the case of pain, infection and fever.

CRYSTAL BALL

Work with crystal balls is reserved for those more advanced in the teaching of crystal therapy and is beyond the scope of this book. However, I can provide a few indications which may be useful for those who already have a ball or would like to acquire one. Incidentally, one needs to purify it more often than other crystals.

Sleeping with a crystal ball is recommended, but you should sleep with it for between six months and a year before working with it. It is enough just to be with it, live with it, have it as a friend, sleep with it and energise it frequently in the appropriate sources of water.

This is the best way of starting work with crystal balls. Do not attempt to crystal gaze for long periods of time as that can be bad for the eyes. Crystalline balls directly stimulate the optic nerve.

In this chapter I have described the stones and crystals with which we work most frequently.

DIFFERENT WAYS
OF WORKING
WITH CRYSTALS

I t is important to stress from the start that crystals or stones cannot do their therapeutic work alone. They simply amplify your own healing energies and intentions.

Each person who works with one or several crystals for healing purposes must be conscious of this fact and make a real effort to breathe and visualise the specific effects they expect from each crystal. By taking a few minutes each day to energise your thought patterns through breathing exercises and visualisation, you will obtain beneficial – and sometimes even spectacular – results with crystals.

Force follows thought, which is the creator. Once expressed, it continues to work, especially when it is strengthened by daily visualisation. It is this force, once oriented according to the specific ray of the crystal prism being used, which can be amplified and channelled continuously through it.

Keeping this objective in mind, we can now study the different ways of using crystals.

You can benefit from the specific vibration of a particular crystal by carrying it on you – in your pocket, for example. However, you must avoid any contact between the crystal and any coins, since they have been touched by many other people. A small pouch can come in useful, either slipped inside a pocket or pinned on to your clothes. Your crystal can also be worn as a piece of jewellery, particularly if metals such as gold or silver are used, since these act as conductors of energy – gold being of the solar type and silver of the lunar type.

Tinctures of a particular stone are made with water which becomes impregnated with the energy, vibration and frequency of the crystal. They are administered internally. The crystal must be coloured so that a definite vibration is present.

For example, you cannot obtain a tincture of clear quartz crystal, because it does not possess a particular vibration; it is universal and can adopt any vibration you give it.

Once the water has acquired the vibration of the desired crystal, add a little alcohol to fix the frequency in the water and to maintain the charge that results. A tincture can be kept indefinitely.

The process is a little like that used in homeopathy or in the preparation of Bach flower remedies. A stone tincture takes about a week to make, followed by a special ceremony for the water which lasts a further seven consecutive days. The dosage is as follows: four to eight drops under the tongue, between two and four times a day or as needed. The tincture reacts within 20 minutes. You should not take any other type of tincture during this period and equally you should not eat any food or take any medicines.

The effect is very quick when a tincture is used because the treatment is internal. When it comes into contact with the mucous membranes under the tongue, the whole body responds to the specific vibration of the crystal being used. When you are working to contain a health problem, the first step is often to administer a tincture because of its strength and the speed with which it takes effect.

Essences made from crystals can also be used. While you need only one day to make these, their charge is not permanent, unlike stone tinctures. Essences will only remain effective for a month. They are less condensed than tinctures, although their effect is the same, and you can easily swallow half or a whole cup in one go. In Chapter Eight you will see how to make essences.

It is also possible to visualise the properties of a particular stone and then to channel the properties, vibrations and colour of that stone towards another person. You can do this work for yourself or for someone else.

Here is a story that may help to make this point clearer.

Aquamarine contains a property that arouses good, harmonious relations between people. One day, a journalist came to see me about an article in a magazine. Our meeting went very well. Some while later, I got in touch with him to find out the result. He told me that the editor had changed his article to such a degree that he had to refuse its publication because he could not accept the amount of alterations she had made.

He was due to have a meeting with her shortly and there was obviously a conflict of personalities between them.

I began to meditate on this and visualised, in their meeting, an aquamarine above their heads which flooded them with its light. The result of the meeting was positive. They listened to each other's point of view patiently and the article was finally published in the way it had originally been written.

This is an example of how a stone's energy can be used through visualisation. It is probably the most simple, but also the most effective, technique if you have carried out the first principle described in the introduction – that of meditation.

You should bear in mind that it is not necessary to wear a crystal on any particular part of your body, with the exception of a protective quartz which should be worn around the spiritual plexus (just like the cornelian which you should wear round the neck for some therapeutic applications). This is because our etheric body – the first electromagnetic field around us which communicates energy – directs the stone's vibrations to the appropriate spot. If, for example, you are suffering with problems around the pancreas and you wear a peridot on your finger, your electromagnetic field will see to it that the energy from this stone is directed to the right place – in this case, the pancreas.

It is equally possible to mix different crystals together – for example, a clear, transparent (and thus colourless) crystal with a coloured one. However you should not mix two crystals of different colours and, as far as possible, you should try to limit individual pieces of jewellery to just one type of crystal. If not, you will not really be able to benefit from the effect of a particular stone.

You can wear several crystals at the same time as long as the different stones are not in the same piece of jewellery and do not touch each other. Metal conducts energy. Therefore, if an item of jewellery carries several stones together, these will cancel each other out – with the exception of a clear crystal and a coloured stone. In the latter case, the transparent crystal will serve to amplify the effect of the coloured one.

PRACTICAL
EXERCISES

ℰ

Here are several experiments you can easily carry out which will help you in your work with crystals, but you must first learn to work with your hands.

Crystals are very powerful tools and it is possible to make mistakes if a)they are wrongly used, b) you are not in a state of perfect balance or c) you are not able to sense correctly the level of healing which the person you are treating can cope with, physically and spiritually. With your hands, however, it is impossible to make such mistakes.

Your hands are natural healing instruments which are adaptable and allow the people you are treating to draw only what they need from you. You cannot subconsciously transmit a harmful force to someone through your hands. It is therefore particularly beneficial to learn how to use your hands properly for healing before working with crystals.

In the cup of your hands there is a secondary chakra which is able to emit and receive at the same time. Some people call it the eye of the hand, because it can see and read. When you hit your knee on the corner of the table, you immediately cover it with your hand because your body knows instinctively that in your hand there is a healing force. When you meet someone close to you who is upset, your first natural gesture is to put your hand on them.

In the first place it is necessary to increase your vital energy so that you will be better equipped to transfer this to the patient. You can compare the phenomenon with an electric wire. A very thin wire will only be able to take a feeble voltage, while a larger one can carry much more.

If you do not possess much vital energy, or your channels or energy circuits are small or blocked, they will only be able to release a small amount of current to help or heal anyone in need. On the other hand, if you have an abundance of vital energy and all your channels are properly open, they will be able to transmit a strong voltage, thus providing a greater healing force and obtaining better results.

In order to increase your vital energy and open up all your channels, you must first consider what you eat. By consuming food that is high in vital energy, you will, over a period of time, increase the vital energy inside yourself. One very simple way of increasing the vital energy in your food is by using your hands.

You must hold them one in front of the other, with the palms turned inwards. By moving them towards and then away from each other, try to notice the sensations that you feel. After a while, you will become aware of a stronger feeling in a certain, precise spot, as if you were holding a ball of energy in your hands. Now rub your hands well, with your elbows out, and blow on them. Carry on doing this until they become warm. Then hold them as before, again moving them towards and away from each other. You will feel your ball of energy increased, almost doubled – and even more in some cases.

This is what has happened. By rubbing your hands together, you have stimulated your secondary chakra in the palm of your hands, which in turn feels and emits more, thus doubling the energy field between them. By rubbing in this way, you have also stimulated the wave nerve, which connects the brain with all the other glands in the human body. This helps balance the two hemispheres of the brain, thus providing you with better perception.

Using this method, you can boost the vital energy of your food before eating it. First you must taste a little bit of every item in silence, taking care to remember the exact taste of each. Then rub your hands together well as described above and place them above your plate while projecting, through your hands, the following thought: 'To help and to cure'. When you feel the ball of energy rising under your hands, this means that your food has assimilated the energy.

As a rule, this operation takes between 30 seconds and a minute. Raw vegetables only need about 15 seconds, while 'fast food' can take as much as 4 minutes. The better the food is for your health, the less time you need to energise it. After doing this, taste each item of food again. You will certainly notice a difference. (If you carry out this test with a glass of water, you will find it easier to notice the difference since water has a very neutral taste.)

With the help of this technique you can find out whether food has gone bad or is poisoned. For example, I will tell you about one experience I had.

I had ordered a plate of sushi chicken and, as is our custom, began by energising the food. However, I did not feel the ball of energy beneath my hands which always confirms that the food has taken the charge. I started again, this time even more focused, but there was nothing I could do. The energy was just not there.

This was the first time this had ever happened to me and, as a result, I did not trust the food very much. I tasted a small piece and immediately got a heavy feeling in my stomach. I immediately decided not to eat the meal. My friend offered to change plates. We did. She did not get any response with her hands either when she tried to energise the plate of chicken, but she ate it all the same. The next day I found out that she had been sick all night.

One of my students had a similar experience. It happened one evening, after a day's course, when she was having her meal with the family. She tried to energise her food, but felt no energy under her hands. She decided not to eat but her husband and daughter did and were both ill during the night.

Therefore, always remember that if your hands do not give you the expected energy response, it is because the food is not good for you. When I go to a restaurant, I energise everything I eat. Sometimes, a single item on the plate does not respond and I do not eat it. In all the years I have practised this technique, I have never suffered from indigestion, food poisoning or any other similar problems – and this despite the fact that in my travels I do from time to time eat in some dubious places.

My advice, particularly to those who are ill or convalescing, is not to eat anything that has not been energised. In order to get well and recuperate, it is important that you eat only food that is good for you. Even medicines can benefit from this practice of energising, with the focused thought: 'To help and to cure'.

It is not necessary always to taste the food before energising it. I would advise you to do it for the first few times so that you can see for yourself how this practice really changes the quality of what you are eating. This practice also pleases the spirits of nature, since they see it as evidence of your respect for them.

Now another important experiment.

First find a tree or plant, then rub your hands to energise them and try to find the electromagnetic field that surrounds it. How far away is this from the tree? Just like us, all vegetation has its own electromagnetic field which varies according to each one. Walk about inside this field and try to sense through your hands the differences you feel around the trunk, the leaves, a notch, perhaps an insect you find on it. Try this on various plants and note the differences.

You are now beginning to work on your perception of fields. Each person will feel something different with their hands. Do not be apprehensive, but pay attention. Discover the subtleties that your hands can detect, but do not go with preconceived ideas or prior expectations.

After experimenting with trees and plants, try the same thing with animals if you can and finally experience the effects with human beings. Ask the person you are working with questions that will help to throw light on your sensations. We all feel differently and the messages we receive through our hands are often unique. We must therefore develop our own personal code and the best way to do that is through questioning a willing helper.

If the texture or the feeling under your hands changes, ask the person involved if they are suffering pain in that spot. This sensation could perhaps correspond to an old injury which has remained 'programmed' in the electromagnetic field. I never cease to be surprised by the great variety of different sensations that people tell me they have felt during this exercise. One feels heat in the affected area, while for another it is cold; one will notice pain in their own hand, while another will feel it in their body; one will notice a rough texture, another a vibration and so on. You must gradually discover and understand your own code.

Also, watch out for fluctuations in the electromagnetic field. Around certain parts of the body it can be denser or thinner. Sometimes there can be holes in it. You should usually rebalance such variations and readjust them (see Chapter Nine: The Therapeutic Touch). For the moment, however, be content just to notice them.

There are other preparatory exercises you can try which are helpful for therapeutic work with crystals and stones. Sleeping with a crystal is one of them. For this you should hold a clear quartz in your hand when you go to bed. It does not matter if it drops out during the night, because in fact the crystal moves around on its own and will naturally find the place where you are suffering from health problems. You will notice this when you wake up, according to where you find the crystal.

Many minor ailments (a sore finger or back, or numbness in the hands) will be cured simply through the crystal's perfection tuning into yours and amplifying your natural state of good health.

Through this experience you will see for yourself how far the crystal, when it is respected and used in the right way, works by itself. You will also see how consciousness is increased through the effect of the crystal. This is why you will get the impression of sleeping less for the first few nights you spend with the crystal, although in fact this is not the case. You are simply more conscious of what is around you, even when you are asleep, and this gives you the impression of not sleeping.

You will also find that you wake up more easily because your awareness is sharper. And, on waking up, you will feel completely rested even though you do not have the impression of having slept well. With time, you will get used to this feeling. During the night, the crystal helps purify the body, attracting to itself the harmful elements that collect alongside the positive ions which have accumulated in the magnetic field during the day. When you wake up, do not forget to put the crystal in salted water to purify it.

I now want to look at a method of concentrating. In order to achieve a holistic understanding and knowledge of life, we have to use the two halves of the brain. This is known as 'focusing oneself'.

The left half senses in a rational, logical, linear and objective way. It is the memory bank and the computer. It is the 'Doubting Thomas' that only believes something when it can actually be seen with the naked eye. The right half senses in an imaginative, emotional, abstract, circular and subjective way. It sees everything as a whole.

The two halves together are essential for comprehension of any situation. It is important to grasp all the facts from an emotional as well as a rational point of view, something our society too often forgets. In the context of therapy, however, one cannot forget this.

You will notice that, when the two halves of the brain are synchronised, you see better, you hear better and you feel better. You are more aware and feel a kind of inner calm which could be called the 'void'.

This interior void allows you to fill yourself with knowledge and energy. If there is no void, then there is no place in which to put anything. If the void exists, it can welcome energy, spiritual and physical, which will inspire you with new ideas and allow you the space to understand them fully.

It is essential to look very carefully at anyone who approaches you for help. You must search for an overall view without being either too subjective or too objective. Your vision and understanding must not be blurred or influenced by your own weaknesses and problems. A non-focused mind tends to create a screen or haze which prevents us from seeing reality clearly.

Take this example of the child and the politician.

The child, whose attitudes have not been warped by life, understands the teacher's meaning as the teacher explains. There is no delay for reflection: the understanding is immediate. As soon as the information reaches the brain, it is absorbed by it. This is what is meant by being focused. The politician, on the other hand, has an ulterior motive: that of being elected or putting across a specific point of view. As soon as anyone with whom he is in discussion expresses an idea, rather than listening and absorbing, a politician tries to use it for his own ends. This creates a kind of screen and prevents him from understanding clearly what the other person is saying. In the same way, you can sometimes see two adults talking together for hours on end without ever really understanding each other, even though they are saying the same thing.

In order to concentrate you should use a special breathing technique to clear and relax the throat. When it is open and relaxed, the chakra in the throat enables the brain's two halves to synchronise and become focused. This method is the quickest and simplest of all those that I have been taught over the years, which is why I recommend it.

First take several deep breaths (at least three) in order to draw plenty of oxygen into your system. During each complete breath you should feel your hands – one placed on the solar plexus and the other on your chest – moving. (If you do not manage this, you must carry out some exercises to increase your respiratory capacity so that your stomach and chest expand when you breathe.) Then breathe in and out slowly through your nose, letting out naturally a little sound from your throat without forcing it. (When you have got into the habit, this will no longer be necessary.)

In the middle of breathing, stop making this sound. You will find your breathing stops as well. During this pause, concentrate on your throat and imagine it is open and relaxed. On no account should your throat be tight. To feel what this is like, take a deep breath and hold it. Can you feel the contraction at the base of the neck? It is this contraction that you must avoid. Your throat must always be open and relaxed, even when you stop breathing. Practise breathing in and out like this three times and each time increase the period during which you hold your breath.

It is not necessary always to make the little throat noise when breathing out. I advise you to make this sound the first time, since it is a way of checking that your throat is perfectly relaxed. Your vocal cords only vibrate when they are relaxed. It will also ensure that you succeed in mastering the technique of concentration. After breathing in and out three times, you will be in a focused state for about forty minutes.

If this practice is carried out correctly, it will put you in a 'focused' state. But to make sure that you have done it properly, take the time to compare your feelings before and after. Before starting the exercise, look at the colours around you, the light, the voices you hear, the sounds, the noises around you and how you perceive other people nearby. Also take time to think about how you yourself feel inside, the state of your inner being at that moment.

Do the exercise as explained above and then compare your feelings. Look at the colours and the light, listen to the sounds around you, observe others and note how you feel inside. If the breathing exercise has been correctly carried out, you should feel more relaxed and calmer and the space around you should appear larger. Colours should look brighter and the sounds and voices around you should seem clearer, more precise and distinct.

The 'void' of which I have spoken has been installed inside you and that means you are 'focused'. You feel better, you are calmer and more relaxed and you see and hear better. In short, all your faculties have been enhanced. Your potential in terms of a human being is available because you are 'focused'; you are truly in the real world. The two halves of your brain are working simultaneously and are perfectly synchronised.

You will notice that if you are focused before you sit an exam, for example, the final results will be better. If you are focused before you put on a show, you will not suffer butter-flies in your stomach. If you are focused before you make an important statement, your message will be understood that much better. If you are focused when someone approaches you in a fit of rage, you will avoid this negative force which will pass right through and not affect you, since the anger will have nowhere to attach itself. If you are focused before providing someone with help, you will see that person better and your energy will be more concentrated.

Because you become more efficient in everything you do, this technique is a prerequisite before any stage of work. Focus yourself before meditating, before officiating at an opening ceremony, before energising your hands to bless the food you eat, before all activity of a therapeutic nature or any important gesture. This way you will obtain the best results.

When you have problems and cannot find a way of solving them, take the time to focus yourself and you will notice that the solutions become self-evident.

When someone who is focused is linked up to a brain scanner, one notices that the brain emits theta waves, reveal-ing a more relaxed state than the usual alpha waves. Theta waves are present in sleep and these wavelengths are very beneficial for concentration, perception and therapeutic treatment.

THE FUNDAMENTAL LAWS OF HEALING AND THE PROGRAMMING OF CRYSTALS

UNCONDITIONAL LOVE

NON-ATTACHMENT

INTENTION

Let us now look at the three fundamental laws of healing. The first one is love – but unconditional love, not that which is generally found in society. I refer especially to love that is not possessive, which does not look to restrain, which gives itself equally to everyone and not more to one than another. Like the sun, this love shines as much for the bad as the good.

Compassion is at the heart of any helping relationship. You must want to help to be able to carry out a treatment that will be beneficial, right and balanced for another person. You must feel this compulsion to help in a spirit of compassion and love.

However, you must be careful not to confuse this understanding of love, which is compassion, with pity. Pity will alienate those you feel sorry for, because when you pity someone, you cannot be comfortable facing their feelings. You suffer when confronted by their suffering, because you want it to stop. On the other hand, with compassion you do not get directly involved in their suffering. Compassion is something detached and there only to give and to share. It is the same for everyone, regardless of the degree of suffering, and has value in every kingdom. It will offer the same strength to the sufferer, be they a person, a plant or an animal.

This compassionate attitude comes from understanding who we are. Through meditation we come to recognise the mystery within. We can then become conscious of the fact that the other person is a reflection of the same mystery. This love in compassion is, at the same time, love of ourselves. It is a matter of giving to another person what we would wish to receive. Through feeling this sense of togetherness – that we are as one – we must learn to share those resources of love that are inside us.

It is clear that this kind of love cannot be expressed without loving oneself. It is only then that one is in a position to love others. We must feel compassion for ourselves before experiencing it with others. That is why this attitude of compassion should accompany any meditation, when we sit in silence and sense the mystery that lives inside us all.

As a therapist, you must give yourself some moments of relaxation and pleasure. I generally advise my students to allocate at least one day a week to doing only those things that they like. It is important for a therapist to be replenished so that they have a well of happiness, well-being and joy to pass on to others, without any loss of energy.

You should therefore enjoy yourself wherever and whenever you can. It is very important to understand that you must look after yourself before trying to look after others. As the saying goes: 'Charity begins at home'. It is only by giving yourself some time to recover, for your own pleasure, joy and well-being, that you will be able to offer these to others and be convincing when you tell them that they too have a right to be healthy and happy and have peace of mind.

The first fundamental principle in any approach to a helping relationship is love, because the healing comes from love. When someone embodies love all over, that person will succeed in healing just by a touch of their fingertips. Such was the case with Jesus Christ, who cured the sick with just a touch of his fingers or through being touched by them, because he was the very embodiment of love. He lived for himself to the point of giving his life on the cross for the remission of the sins of humanity.

It is of little importance what method one uses for healing, whether it be homeopathy, crystal therapy, polarity, phytotherapy, psychotherapy or traditional medicine. Love is always the first fundamental law. It is not so much the technique employed which is effective, but rather the ability of the therapist to embody those basic truths necessary for healing – that is to say, the three fundamental laws.

The second fundamental law of healing is non-attachment, which follows on from the first law. As I have already explained, pity is a sentiment that is attached, while compassion involves absolutely no attachment.

The non-attachment signifies that you are not linked to the result and you understand that it is the other person who is responsible for their own cure. It is never the therapist who heals the other person. You are only a tool, a channel, an instrument in the healing process. The best therapist and the best medicine in the world will not be able to heal someone who does not want to be healed. The illness will remain or move to another spot, but it will not disappear because the patient has decided to keep it, whether consciously or otherwise.

You must fully understand that a therapist is not a god, and the only person responsible for a cure is the one affected. This is why you should not be linked to the result. If that person gets better, you must not feel proud and boast about the cure. Equally, if that person does not get better, you should not blame yourself, feel guilty and run yourself down.

This principle of non-attachment is, in fact, an insurance for the therapist and guarantees that they will always be objective, impartial and well balanced. It is the patient who will succeed in curing himself. And you must not forget, either, that illness is an opportunity for growth, a signal that tells us we must change and restore our harmony with the universe. Considered in this light, illness becomes a less negative affair which can be healthy for our evolution.

We must sometimes accept that the cure for someone may actually involve death, which is itself a stage of growth, a transition. The therapist will come across cases where people have finished their time in this life and the role of the therapist will be to lead them to death, help them to die. However, it is essential that in such a case the individual is allowed to progress naturally. Herein lies one of the great problems of allopathic medicine, because it tries by all means possible to keep people alive, even when this conflicts with their time to die. We all know the suffering that this can cause both family and patient.

In such a case, the therapist should not work on the illness, but on the person affected. You should strengthen and help their sense of evolution and development.

This understanding brings us to the third fundamental law, which is intention. Having a clear intention of what you want to achieve is fundamental to all therapeutic applications. Energy follows the thought, which is a little like an electric wire carrying the healing current.

Imagining clearly the intention of the treatment will help the therapist to use to the full the healing energy, whether this is in the form of a crystal, medicines, acupuncture, massage or simply advice. If you know how to keep clearly in mind your intention to heal, the results will be all the more positive and beneficial.

However, here is an example of an intention that is inappropriate and will not benefit the patient: 'I want to reduce the suffering, soothe the pain and cure the illness'. This intention is bad because what stands out is 'suffering', 'pain' and 'illness'. Importance is being given to the problem. However it is not the problem that you should be energising, but rather the person – by giving them strength to help relieve them of the health problems they are experiencing.

Here is an example of a good intention: 'This person is showing perfect health, the forces are circulating freely throughout their body and they feel absolutely fine'. By imagining this intention, the healing energy will follow the thought, the channel that you have prepared for it, and the patient will be better equipped to use, in a beneficial way, the energy that is available through you at that moment.

Everything is in the intention. For example, when energising your food, if you forget to concentrate on the intention 'To help and to cure', you will know it soon enough. The effect of this practice will be greatly reduced, your digestion will not be so good and the taste of the food will be less enhanced.

So all rests in the intention that you put into the gesture. Just making the gesture is not sufficient. The effectiveness of your work depends on the intention you attach to it. You must orientate the energy, because natural energy will react in an erratic way and it must be directed with the aim of being beneficial. It is your intention that enables the energy to be orientated.

This, then, is the third fundamental law of healing: intention.

It can be useful to know exactly what is wrong with the person being treated in order to arrive at the right intention. But you must be careful not to mention it. In effect, the better informed you are of the problem to be treated, the more able you will be to orientate the energy correctly and to make it work in the patient's favour, because you will understand and know where to direct it.

On the other hand, diagnosing someone's illness by confirming its existence, for example by saying: 'You have got cancer', will only reinforce the belief of the patient in the illness. His cancer, his illness, will be strengthened by this. Therefore it is important to understand that in fact the illness does not exist. It is just a hindrance, an alarm signal in the life of the person affected. It amounts to a transitory state, which the individual either sinks into or escapes from.

Of course it is good to know the illness thoroughly, what type of cancer it is, what it is attacking, what the effects are and so on. And for that one has to name it, but it is not good to confirm the existence of the illness in fatalistic terms or to talk about it in such a way near the patient. You must learn how to choose your words carefully and allow the energy to circulate in a way that will be helpful for the cure.

You must never forget that the illness does not really exist, that it is transitory. In fact, we do not exist either, because we are also transitory. We are continually in a state of change. In reality, the 'Luc Bourgault' now will not be the same in two seconds' time. Behind all physical manifestation there is a kind of void which is the non-manifested potential of all that exists. It is, in a way, what we call the spiritual world.

PROGRAMMING A CRYSTAL

Having understood these principles, you will be in a position to prepare your intentions correctly for programming crystals. To programme a crystal you must, in the first place, be focused. To do this, practise conscientiously the procedure explained at the end of the previous chapter.

Once you are focused, take the crystal in your hands,

establish your intention (its creation) and then breathe it directly on to the crystal (its manifestation) while holding it in your cupped hands, which you should put up to your mouth. This gesture is found in several of the myths about the creation of the world, where God created man by breathing on the clay statuettes that he made so that they could come to life.

In doing this, your breath will impregnate the crystal with your intention and activate it. This intention will then rest in the crystal for about 28 days or until you purify it in salted water. When you have reached a more advanced level, you will be able to learn how to programme a crystal permanently. But that is beyond the scope of this book.

A crystal can house several intentions (a maximum of four or five) as long as they are compatible. Programming the sun and the moon, for example, in the same crystal is incompatible, whereas water and the moon are compatible.

COLOURS AND
THEIR PROPERTIES

The three primary colours (blue, red and yellow) symbolise the three attributes of the divine on a physical level. Blue represents the will to be, to live and to exist in a physical body; red represents love, compassion, devotion or the emotional being; and yellow corresponds to spirit, creative intelligence or the intellectual being.

Fundamental energy, clear light, breaks down into seven colours as it passes through a prism or a cloud of raindrops. Each colour orientates energy in a well-determined fashion.

The first three colours of the rainbow (red, orange and yellow) are the warm colours. Green is the neutral colour, at the same time both stimulating and calming; it represents balance. The last three colours of the rainbow (blue, indigo and violet) are the cold colours.

In the case of chronic illness (which lasts for some time), there is usually a lack of energy. In such instances, you should generally use a warm colour to provide energy. Where the illness is acute (and sudden), it is the opposite; there is too much energy concentrated in the body. This happens when, for example, one has a headache, is burnt or has an accident. Under the effect of shock, lots of blood and energy accumulate around the wound. Here you should use a cold colour, which will have the effect of calming, relaxing and making the energy circulate.

For all illnesses where you have to find a balance, you should work with the colour green. This is, in every way, a safe colour. If you are in any doubt, use green. It is the colour of healing. Good health is a state of equilibrium and green symbolises it. Moreover, therapists often have a lot of green in their aura, since their mission is to restore the balance in the people they treat.

Let us analyse briefly the specific properties of each colour.

RED

This is the colour of love, of passion and of the vital force that constructs, that builds. It is of instantaneous energy, which has a direct influence on the etheric centre which governs physical vitality. It is the colour that feeds the living forces of the body, the blood and the immune system. Red enlivens and energises. It symbolises fire, heat, anger and materialisation on a physical level.

Since this colour is very powerful, we must always use it with caution. When red is employed in treatments, it must always be balanced afterwards with green or blue. Some drivers even use a tincture of ruby when they want to stop themselves falling asleep. When a few drops of this tincture are put under the tongue, the effect is immediate and they are completely awake.

There are, however, limits as far as its consumption is concerned. It would be absurd to take it every 20 minutes, for example. Our body needs to stop every so often and sleep. Moreover, an overdose of the tincture can be harmful. It is a little like the effect you get from amphetamines.

Summary

Red stimulates and strengthens. It arouses action, creation and construction on the physical level. It is the colour of the heart and the small intestine. On an emotional level, it stirs up love, passion and devotion.

ORANGE

This is the colour that recharges the etheric body and enables the physical body to use available forces properly. It transmits the vital energy. Certain religious sects wear this colour and their adherents have a tendency towards excess, whether it be concerned with sex, diet or whatever, in their desire to profit from life to the maximum. Orange helps them by continually redistributing their energies and, in this way, the excesses they indulge in do not harm them unduly.

The colour orange is effective from the point of view of the digestive system and also helps to eliminate surplus bodily forces. It is a co-ordinator and distributor of energy and is useful in the process of elimination, assimilation and procreation in a way that is less strong and more balanced than with the colour red. It is stimulating and positive.

Summary

Orange co-ordinates and controls energy. It has a liberating effect which decrystallises that which has been repressed. On a physical level, it is the colour of the stomach, the spleen and the pancreas. The energy of this colour facilitates the assimilation and distribution of food. On an emotional level, it encourages good humour, enthusiasm and a warm atmosphere.

YELLOW

From an energy point of view, yellow works on more subtle levels. It carries an element of psychological tonic. It feeds the brain, the nervous system, the stomach, the spleen, the pancreas, the eyes, the nails and the hair. This colour is also energising, although it is more subtle and influences the superior mind and the soul.

Summary

Yellow is clarity and light. It is a colour of action and opening. It feeds the nervous system and cleans and purifies the whole of the physical body. It acts in a beneficial way on the skin. Yellow helps with emotional balance and develops and enriches the brain in its intellectual functions.

GREEN

As for green, this gives us equilibrium. It is both calming and energising. It encourages harmony, good health, well-being and unity. It creates a calm which does not impede activity and it exercises a great and positive influence on the heart and blood circulation. If you do not know what colour to use, you cannot go wrong with green. It is the colour of healing and is always beneficial. That is why nature is dressed in green. It restores tired nerves. It is the colour of the liver and the gallbladder.

Summary

Green is the most beneficial colour in the industrialised world. It creates balance, harmony, healing and peace. It is a neutral colour which is neither warm nor cold. It calms, refreshes and tones up the body on all levels. It helps in the healing of the heart and good blood circulation.

BLUE

The colour blue is soothing, refreshing, astringent and disinfecting. It reduces inflammation and fever and assists relaxation and sleep. It is, for example, the ideal colour for your bedroom ceiling. It symbolises music and rules the chakra of the throat. In hospitals surgeons wear blue-green, since blue carries disinfecting qualities while green allows them to remain stable and balanced.

Summary

Blue is a refreshing, astringent and disinfecting colour. It creates emotional stability and mental clarity. Loyalty and truth are associated with it. Blue opens the spirit to understanding and spiritual perception and it helps organise thought, expression and communication.

INDIGO

This colour takes us to even deeper levels of relaxation. It carries inspiration and intuition and rules the pineal gland. It is the colour of the kidneys and the bladder. Indigo induces sleep and works on the areas of the lungs, the nose, the sinuses, the ears, the mouth and the throat. Any spiritual application involving devotion will generally be helped by indigo.

Summary

Indigo is a very soothing colour which increases all one's

faculties of perception. It helps sleep, silence and meditation and leads to deep religious sentiments and devotion. On an emotional level, it corresponds with serenity. Indigo is beneficial for any problems involving the kidneys, sinuses, eyes and throat.

VIOLET

The seventh colour – violet – is that of spiritual control. On a physical level it has a particular tendency to soothe, while on a mental or spiritual level it stimulates. Violet symbolises transformation and transmutation and it is used when working with psychic illnesses such as neurosis, psychosis, epilepsy and cerebral and glandular problems. It rules the pituitary gland. It leads to more elevated levels of conscience.

Summary

Violet has the most elevated vibration of all the colours of the prism. It creates spiritual purification, the transmutation of negative emotions, mental relaxation and transformation towards a more refined and subtle being. It also leads towards the essence of the being. It harmonises the body, which is then better able to assimilate the prana (energy) of the universe. It works especially on the superior levels of the being.

PINK

Pink contains both white (purity) and red (love) and symbolises the unconditional love that will be useful when working on problems of the heart.

Summary

Pink is the colour of love and compassion. It eases anger and negative emotions. It is the energy of the rose quartz.

WHITE

The colour white symbolises purity and virginity. It is the colour of the lungs and the colon. It is not the white light one talks about when one refers to that light which gives birth to all the colours. That light, in which the whole luminous spectrum is contained, is clear. It was wrongly believed that this was the colour white, but the error arose from a mistranslation of the expression 'clear light' in Sanskrit, which was translated as 'white light'.

We cannot see through white, because it is opaque. We could not see through a window that was white. Only if it was clear would we be able to see through it. The light of the sun is clear, not white. When we talk of surrounding ourselves in light for protection, we mean clear light. If we surrounded ourselves in white light, we would not be in such a good position to join in with the universe and receive those forces that are favourable. Because white light is opaque, it cuts out certain forces.

Summary

White is purifying and stablising to the whole of a person's energy system.

BLACK

Black light – or what some shamans call the 'spiritual' light – is another kind of light. To use or 'consult' the black light, these medicine men carry out certain rituals by which they must eliminate all other sources of light. It is a spiritual light that leads to the source of all non-manifested potential. Most of the black stones have a tendency to absorb negativity, to assimilate it and thus protect us from the harmful influences that they have captured.

Summary

Black is a protective colour. It is also grounding. However, use in moderation and always use in conjunction with another colour.

The particularities of different colours that I have just described do not replace their sensation. It is important to 'feel' the effect of the colours, since only by direct experience will you receive all the information that is integrated in them. When you feel what the colour reveals to you, without any intellectual thought, you can use its therapeutic effects with greater precision and you will be in a better position to visualise the colour properly.

To 'feel' the effect of a colour, I advise you to meditate while you impregnate yourself with that colour. For example, breathe in a red light for a few minutes and note carefully how your body reacts to the colour. Follow this with further exercises, using other colours. This kind of meditation exercise will give you a true understanding of the different colours used in therapy.

COLOURS AND THEIR CONNECTIONS TO STONES

Here is a description of the stones connected with each colour and the illnesses and symptoms that they can treat.

RED

Stimulating and energising
1st chakra
Note: do

The red ray can be used, in general, for the following areas: anaemia, problems involving blood cell deficiency, eczema, sciatica, fractures, depression, fatigue, despondency, cancer, lumbago and paralysis. It helps stimulate the five senses.

WARNING: Never use red without ending the treatment by cooling the body with green or blue – especially in the case of cancer.

Red Ray Crystals and their Characteristics

Ruby: Improves circulation; treats blood deficiencies such as anaemia; increases haemoglobin; eases digestion; raises temperature; stimulates energy levels in a general way.

Garnet: Must be faceted to give off its energy. Works on the same level as ruby but is more gentle and less vibrant. Start with a garnet before using a ruby.

Pink quartz: For all problems concerning the heart, whether emotional or physical. Put it near babies when they are upset or give it to them as a toy (big enough not to be swallowed); used for calming, soothing and relaxing – particularly hyperactive children.

ORANGE

Stimulating and revitalising
2nd chakra
Note: re

The orange ray can be used, in general, for the following areas: teeth and bones, asthma, bronchitis and lung problems; liver and kidneys, loss of vitality, recharging the etheric body; recommended for nervous tension and exhaustion, boils, phobias and inhibitions; helps digestion.

Orange Ray Crystals and their Characteristics

Citrine: The 'coyote' stone, because it works even on the most stubborn and resistant to treatment. Excellent crystal for single-minded people with fixed ideas. Purifies the density in the 5th field. Start with 'madeira' citrine (very deep orange, almost brown) and when the effect is clearly underway use the golden citrine.

Cornelian agate: For blockages to the chakra of the throat; for difficulties with expression.

YELLOW

Stimulating and illuminating
3rd chakra
Note: mi

The yellow ray can be used, in general, for the following areas: stimulating the brain, the intellect and both the physical and etheric vision; good for the gall-bladder, liver, skin (texture, scars), constipation, diabetes and dyspepsia; stimulates the heart and builds up nerves and muscles; eliminates intestinal parasites; removes calcium deposits in those suffering from arthritis; excellent for treating colds and mucus.

Yellow Ray Crystals and their Characteristics

'Champagne' topaz, golden topaz and golden citrine: They share the forces of 'madeira' citrine, but softer.

Golden beryl and peridot: These are green stones, but they also have a yellow ray. They share the properties of the two colours.

GREEN

Sedating, relaxing and rhythmic
4th chakra
Note: fa

The green ray can be used, in general, for the following areas: heart problems, arterial pressure, kidneys, bladder, gall-bladder, nervous tension and migraine; stimulates the pituitary gland (in fact, all the glands); boosts vitality; dissolves blood clots; eliminates toxins; frees congestion in crowded cells; treats cancer, diarrhoea, ulcers and hypo-glycaemia.

Green Ray Crystals and their Characteristics

Emerald: Regenerates tired nerves; beneficial for all affections which involve the need to restore equilibrium. (All green stones contribute equally in this respect.)

Green tourmaline and tsavorite: Green garnet.

Peridot: Can stimulate and balance at the same time, because it possesses both yellow and green. For depression, obesity, constipation, ulcers and prostrate problems.

Dioptase: High blood pressure.

All the green stones can be used for Parkinson's disease, particularly dioptase.

BLUE

Electric and soothing
5th chakra (throat)
Note: sol

The blue ray can be used, in general, for the following areas: inflammation; for unwinding and relaxing; throat infections, jaundice, bilious attacks, fever, skin troubles (itching, burns, cuts and stings), heart palpitations, goitre, colic, female disorders, ulcers and cramp; is antiseptic and congeals the blood.

Blue Ray Crystals and their Characteristics

Aquamarine: Prostate.

Celestite: This is very effective for migraines and headaches. Use it by placing it on the head or by making an essence or tincture (either drunk or applied directly to the skin).

Azurite: WARNING: Do not use this stone in essence form as it gives off sulphur. Effective for bone cancer, tendon problems and fractures.

Blue garnet and opal: Do not use fire opal when you want to work with the blue ray. Amplifies the feminine nature of the body.

Turquoise: Is not a crystal. Represents the sky and its spiritual qualities.

Chrysocoll and malachite: Are used to reduce and eliminate fear.

INDIGO

Self-knowledge and wisdom
6th chakra
Note: la
The indigo ray can be used, in general, for the following areas: eye, ear and nose problems; cataracts, deafness, dyspepsia, swellings, intense pains and tonsillitis; stops haemorrhages; treats nervous and mental disorders; purifies the blood and eliminates radiation; treats asthma, tuberculosis, pneumonia and other lung problems; recommended for opening the mind.

Indigo Ray Crystals and their Characteristics

Deep aquamarine and sapphire: Deep colour including star sapphire; benefits sleep; for eye, ear and nose problems, cataracts, inflammation, uterine tumours, eczema, acne and all lung troubles.

VIOLET

Stimulating and purifying
7th chakra
Note: si
The violet ray can be used, in general, for the following

areas: stress and nervousness; reduces high blood pressure; good against insomnia and epilepsy; reconstructs the white blood corpuscles; depresses lymph and motor nerves; used for mental disorders and spleen problems; stimulates artists and creators; reduces appetite (diet); works as heart depressor and treats shock, rheumatism and neuralgia.

Violet Ray Crystals and their Characteristics

Alexandrite, violet garnet and amethyst: WARNING: Do not use amethyst on hyperactive children, schizophrenics, neurotics or people who are retarded or single-minded; use it for powerful transformations as it represents the processes of alchemy on all bodily matters; overcomes former harmful habits (alcohol and others); can be used for protection; works around the central nervous system and meditation with amethyst clarifies identification or sexual identity. It can be used in musical therapy.

THE SYMBOLISM
OF THE PLANETS

The links between the planetary and astral influences and those of the mineral kingdom are numerous. Planets can be considered as gigantic spherical crystals composed of a very large number of minerals. They all have their own character and have inspired in the human psyche a symbolism that has been enriched over the centuries.

Certainly the vibrations that come from the planets are real and influence both human beings and stones. Unfortunately it is very difficult to measure the concrete influence that the stars exercise, save in the case of the moon and the sun, whose proximity and visibility in our sky have made it possible to gauge their effects on vegetable, animal and human life. Several crystals come to us from different brothers and sisters of Mother Earth.

Sun

This is the dispenser of vitality, the source of heat and light which gives life to all beings on Earth and within the solar system. The sun represents the Divine Fire, the Heavenly Father and will. It is an inexhaustible battery to which we can connect up to nourish every layer of our being. It is the flamboyant Christ that gives equal love to all. It is the model that points the way that leads to knowledge and wisdom.

Its affinities with the mineral world are gold, topaz and ruby. In the body, it represents the heart and the blood. On the question of character, it symbolises loyalty, courage, kindness, generosity and freedom.

All stones are influenced by the sun. Direct contact with the sun's rays stimulates and augments the stone's energy in its solar attributes. When one makes jewellery with a translucent or transparent stone, it is good to leave an opening in the metal under the stone so that the sun's rays can pass through and penetrate the body through the skin. The solar energy is directed in the manner of a prism. The solar ray is thus 'tinted' or 'impregnated' by the mineral frequency.

Moon

This is the soothing, cool and mysterious freshness of the night light. The moon is imagination, gestation, water, the woman's cycles, intuition and fertility – of the body and the Earth. It symbolises the empty uterus which will give form to the solar spirit. It is the void, the unconscious where one senses imprecise and unfinished shapes.

This planetary body is a reflection of the instinctive and emotional nature of the terrestrial kingdoms. It gives a force that materialises, consolidates and structures the creative forces at work in stones, plants, birds and human beings. It is the complement of the sun. Its beauty and light help quiet and gentle meditation.

The American Indians call it 'Grandmother' because, like a wise woman, it watches over everything involved in childbirth.

The stones that are influenced by the moon work in balancing emotions and the body cycles. A crystal's exposure to the moon's rays can bring supplementary energy for precise work connected to the moon's attributes. One must always use this procedure with care, especially if the patient's psychic equilibrium is precarious. Its colour is opalescent and its affinities in the mineral kingdom are moonstone, pearl and silver.

Mars

This is the warrior who tackles challenges and obstacles with force and determination. In Roman mythology Mars was the god of war. The planet's symbol is action. It represents virile, manly, irascible strength.

Mars rules the vein circulation and the spleen. Stimulation, energy, progress, aggression, impulsiveness, speed and leadership are its attributes. Whatever is influenced by the negative side of Mars is passed on by means of excess, anger, egoism or indifference to others.

Mars is a little like the sun, but more frustrated and less luminous. Its connections in the mineral kingdom are cornelian, garnet and iron. Its colour is deep red.

Venus

The lovely and gentle Venus, goddess of beauty, is the mistress of Mars and represents beauty, simplicity, the arts, sensuality, carnal love, maternal feelings, subtlety, gentleness and compassion. Here we find taste (the pleasures of eating), culture, refinement, delicate sentiments and courteous love.

Venus is the female flesh which leads to self-projection through the intensity of desire it engenders in men. It is the sister and the morning star for the planet Earth.

The stones that are influenced by Venus create equilibrium and harmony. Its mineral connections are aquamarine, amethyst and copper.

Mercury

This is the messenger of the gods which, with its winged feet and carrying a wand in its left hand, has become the symbol of medicine. Mercury is lively, swift, light and mischievous. The qualities it transmits are clarity, research, eloquence, finesse and artistic sense. One associates the nervous temperament of the mercurian with travellers, merchants, musicians and doctors.

Mercury develops the mental and intellectual functions. It creates the ability to adapt, the spirit of invention, but also guile and superficiality. It is a ferment of evolution, a leaven which pushes man towards new horizons.

From a mineral point of view, its connections are citrine, opal and mercury (quicksilver). Its colours are changeable and, like itself, difficult to grasp.

Jupiter

This is the largest planet in our solar system and, in Roman mythology, Jupiter is the king, the sovereign of the gods. Its qualities are expansion, authority, material and spiritual wealth, power, influence, generosity and justice. It incarnates both guide and judge.

Stones containing a jupiterian influence improve circulation, distribution and inspiration and raise the body and spirit through the energetic generosity of their impulse. In the body, Jupiter rules the liver. Its stones are blue garnet and royal amethyst and its metal is tin. Royal blue is its colour.

Saturn

Saturn contracts, retains and crystallises and it is said that the lords of karma live there. It is destiny and the law's executor and it creates discipline, order and philosophy. Saturn is the governor, the stabiliser of our solar system, the master who teaches and leads.

The saturnian qualities of endurance, immobility and crystallisation are the very essence of the mineral kingdom and all evolved gems are influenced by Saturn. Its mineral affinities lie with sapphire, obsidian and lead, a heavy and impenetrable metal. Its colour is violet.

Uranus

This is the thundering lightning which smashes to pieces and crystallises. Uranus creates forces that are necessary for the transformation of our society, currently so deeply set in martian passions. It is the planet of Aquarius. It awakens, liberates and puts into motion. It is unpredictable and irrational. Named after Urania, the goddess of astrology, it is the planet of discovery, invention and intuition.

Its mineral affinities lie with quartz crystal, azurite and uranium and its colour is white.

Neptune

This is the upper octave of Venus, the mystic planet named after the god of moisture, seas and oceans. Neptune is the dream, illumination, sacrifice and faith, but also illusion, mirage, drugs, neurosis and imprisonment.

Neptune creates self-sacrifice and develops talent and spiritual perception. Its stones are labradorite and jadeite and its colour is indigo.

Pluto

This is the last planet to be discovered – in 1930 – and the furthest from the sun. This mysterious planet is named after the mythological guardian of hell. Pluto purifies by means of violence and changes in the dark. It represents sexuality, hidden things, the occult and initiation.

Its regenerating power is so strong that it is just as capable of destroying as constructing if it meets with opposition or resistance. It leads towards transmutation of negativity to create a brighter and more spiritual world – and that despite man and his tendencies.

Pluto's stone is black tourmaline and its metal is plutonium. Its colour is black.

BIRTH AND ARTIFICIAL STONES

Birth Stones

The practice of attributing a stone or crystal to each month of the year – the so-called birth stones – is driven by economic criteria rather than by a genuine matching of energies. Business is the origin of this monthly chart of gems – to help undecided purchasers in their choice of jewel.

Therefore, I do recommend that you trust your own intuition more than this chart as far as your choice of jewellery is concerned. You will also notice that there are actually several different charts which do not allocate the same stones to the same months!

Artificial Stones

With the progress of science and technology, the physical and chemical conditions under which crystals are formed can be reproduced in the laboratory. Industry is now in a position to create the majority of precious stones such as the diamond, ruby, sapphire, crystal quartz and emerald.

From an industrial point of view, this is very useful and enables us to produce at an affordable price items such as saws with diamond or sapphire cutting edges. The electronics industry is also able to use synthetic minerals which would otherwise be too costly.

A natural stone takes a lot more time to develop in the bosom of the Earth. Its slow formation and the innumerable telluric and cosmic forces which pass through it in the course of its crystallisation are important factors in its energy structure.

A stone's therapeutic role can only be fully attained in a crystal that has matured slowly in the bosom of Mother Earth. So you will understand why artificial stones are not used in therapeutic treatment.

HOW TO PREPARE ESSENCES AND THE BODY'S ELECTROMAGNETIC FIELDS

୧

To make stone essences, you must first have a clear glass bowl which you should fill with natural or distilled water. You must carry this outside or near to an open window in the morning, with the crystal from which you want to obtain the essence. Ideally choose a day when there is plenty of sunshine. Of course, it is always possible to make an effective essence, even when the weather is cloudy, since the sun is present all the same. But a sunny day is preferable.

If you do not have the crystal you want, programme a clear quartz with the quality of the stone you wanted to use. This means putting two programmes in the crystal: one for the stone you wanted to use and one for your particular intention towards the person for whom you are preparing the essence.

Now sit down and focus yourself. Energise your hands, take hold of the crystal and programme it. Then place it in the bowl of water. Re-energise your hands and hold them under the water while you send out your programming and your intention via your hands into the water. The more specific your intention is, the better the result will be.

Send out your particular intention through your hands into the water. It will take longer than when energising food, between three and five minutes. As with food, when you feel some force, some pressure rising up under your hands, this means there is sufficient charge. At this point, turn your hands clockwise three times and then withdraw them quickly. Your hands act as magnets and attract the forces.

Cover up the bowl with a piece of cloth to protect your water from dust or insects which could otherwise get into it.

Then let the bowl rest in the sun, preferably the whole day or at least for three hours. Finally, take out the crystal and bottle up the liquid you have obtained, storing it in the refrigerator.

The essence can be kept for about a month. After that time, the charge will disappear slowly, making the essence less effective. You can drink it in large quantities, a glass at a time, without any harmful effects.

Here is an example of the use to which you can put these essences. Always keep three or four in the refrigerator of both cold and warm colours. If one of your guests is stressed or nervous, prepare them an infusion with some aquamarine water. That will calm them down considerably. On the other hand, if your guest is depressed and lethargic, this time prepare an infusion with ruby or cornelian water.

Tinctures, unlike essences, take a lot longer to make. They are more concentrated and you need to add some alcohol to retain the charge. A tincture can be kept indefinitely.

The essences of Bach flower remedies are similar to tinctures, the difference being that they contain a little plant element suspended in the liquid. Obviously you do not find elements of crystal in the water, since stones do not dissolve. Bach flower remedies are used more for emotional conditions, whereas crystal or stone essences work better on physical problems.

ELECTROMAGNETIC FIELDS

We will look now at the different electromagnetic fields of the human body.

The first field extends from 15 to 20 centimetres around the body and is called the etheric-physical field. It corresponds to the vital energy and you can see it as rosy lines around the body.

The second field, known as the astral field, extends from the first 30 to 45 centimetres around the body. It is seen as electrical charges, points or circles of colour around the first field. It is this field that people see when they observe the colours of the aura.

The mental-inferior is the third field, which extends around the second. It reveals itself through pale yellow moving lines and represents the objective, linear and rational mind.

The fourth field surrounds the third and is called the mental-superior field or the principle of the soul. It is seen as little green clouds and represents the subjective spirit, the abstract thought, intuition, inspiration, creativity and conscience. It is, in fact, your personality. It is a mixture of your feelings and your thoughts and that is why it is called the principle of the soul.

The spiritual field is the fifth one – also known as the causal field. It corresponds to the spirit of your being, the eternal part of you. It appears as blue and violet moving fingers which penetrate into all the other fields. They set off from the outside of the fourth field and enter through all the other fields as far as the physical body. This is the fusion of the cosmic and the individual, the communion of your being with the powers and forces of the universe.

The sixth and seventh fields do not belong to the individual. Certain spiritual schools consider them as individual manifestations. But we regard them as the fields of cosmic reality, whether a human being is present or not. These fields will manifest themselves (be visible) especially around very developed people, like Christ or Buddha.

In the first stages of therapeutic work, you must evaluate the first field. To do this, you need initially to approach the patient's hands to feel the resistance of his etheric field, about 15 to 20 centimetres from his body. At this distance, the back of the hand is in the astral field. You will thus be able to notice the forces in the astral field, which are often responsible for the patient's problems. You will also be able to feel all the problems present in the physical body in the first field, and sometimes even sense the emotional causes that could be responsible for these troubles. When you reach a more advanced level, you will be able to evaluate the other fields.

It is possible that a person can be completely outside himself, that is to say that his etheric body has moved to one side of him. The individual would then feel very bad in himself. Other states of deficiency can be linked to an imbalance of the etheric field, which can be more or less deep around certain parts of the body. Holes can appear in the etheric field, which give rise to infections, colds and flu, and the 'possession' or catching of emotions that belong to others. We will see how to work with such conditions in the following chapter.

THE THERAPEUTIC TOUCH

ℰ

The therapeutic touch enables you to transmit energy in a beneficial way, once you have acquired good control over the energy exchange beforehand by working with crystals.

The crystal amplifies the energy and this can cause other problems or aggravate existing ones in the patient if the therapeutic touch has not been well mastered. On the other hand, therapeutic work with the hands will enable you to effect successful treatment quickly and in any circumstance. Hands have the advantage of always being with you, wherever you may be, and the therapeutic touch is the form of healing that comes closest to work with crystals. When one adds a crystal to the treatment, the process is simply strengthened.

The therapeutic touch was so named by Dolores Krieger, who studied one of the best known and oldest forms of healing in the world – the 'laying on of hands'. With the information she gained from different healers, and written testimonials concerning this type of healing, she formulated a therapeutic approach that is now practised by thousands of nurses in American hospitals. (Dolores KRIEGER, PhD, RN, *The Therapeutic Touch: How to Use your Hands to Help and to Heal*, Prentice-Hall Inc., New York, NY, 1979.) Of a simplicity matching its effectiveness, this technique offers a rapid means of helping and healing and can assist in a holistic understanding of the quartz crystal approach to therapy.

The techniques used by the great healers over the centuries are similar to those proposed for the therapeutic touch. You must understand that certain individuals have more vital energy to transmit than others and that within this there are very pure channels, clear passages through which the energy of the Holy Mother and the Heavenly Father runs. Thanks to this technique, you can obtain spectacular results. I have already seen hundreds and even thousands of people treated in a single day.

This means of treating and helping patients is nevertheless within everyone's grasp. In almost all cases, it is possible to achieve an improvement, relaxation and a greater sense of well-being in the person being treated.

The therapeutic touch has only one contraindication: **Do not treat an area directly affected by cancer.** There are no other contraindications with the therapeutic touch. This method of treatment can be used for all types of illnesses, all kinds of people and in all circumstances and there is no danger in practising it more than once in the same day. There is, however, just one precaution to take: the treatment should not last more than 30 minutes at any one time.

The therapeutic touch is quick to carry out, since the energy exchanged with the hands is instantaneous. The only negative effect is that it causes some fatigue both to you and your patient. With practice, however, you will become stronger and more resistant, particularly if you specialise in this type of therapeutic approach.

To practise the therapeutic touch, you must first put your hands under cold water. Then focus yourself according to the technique I have described in Chapter Four. Next imagine roots of light disappearing from your feet into the ground. This will enable all surplus energy to become rooted. This way, if your patient releases bad or harmful forces as a result of the treatment and your body receives them, they will not remain there. They will pass through your body into the ground, thanks to the roots of light you have created. This way you do not retain anything that could harm you. It is not even necessary to be standing on firm ground to imagine these roots of light. They will be just as effective if you are on the twentieth floor of a building.

Next imagine a dome of clear light or amethyst above you and the person on whom you are working. This is to protect you since you must open yourself up to exchange forces between each other. Imagine this dome being large enough for you to be able to move around your patient without any problem while remaining inside it. Finally, energise your hands by rubbing them hard one against the other.

Move your hands towards the person being treated until you feel some resistance. This enables you to assess the depth of the etheric field and gives you an indication of the patient's state of health. If, for example, the field is very thin, that can signify that the patient is suffering from allergies or energy deficiency. You should then recharge the etheric field (by visualising, during the treatment, the orange light that recharges the etheric-physical body).

Next, assess the whole of the individual's body, following the edge of the first field and questioning it when you come across any anomalies. You will sometimes find that the field is deeper and stronger in certain spots and thinner and weaker in others. Some holes in the etheric tissue may also be present, which you will notice as a sudden absence of field at a particular spot. It is as you feel these changes in sensation under your hands that you must question the patient to find out what is happening at this precise place. It is good to remember that a problem will often arise in the field before settling in the body. You must therefore have confidence in what your hands detect, even if the patient denies having a problem in the spot where you can feel irregularities.

Once you have made your evaluation – the most accurate possible – of the whole body through this procedure, think about the kind of intention you want to formulate deep down inside; it is this intention which you will be using in your treatment (exchanging energy). Once you have chosen and determined your intention, depending on the problems you have detected (and I suggest you work with the colours for this), begin scanning the patient's etheric field as though you were stroking it. To do this, pass your hands all round the field with gentle, enveloping movements. This will have the effect of soothing the patient and softening the 'texture' of the etheric field.

It is during this stage that you must also re-balance certain parts of the field that are not in harmony (unfocused, too deep, too thin or unbalanced). To do this, you have to shape the field with the help of gestures and breathing and readjust it by pulling or pushing to give it the ideal shape. You can, for example, pull it by breathing in or push it by breathing out.

Then complete the scan and evaluate the results obtained.

When this operation is over, you must shake your hands, because they work a little like crystals and attract the positive ions present in the patient's electromagnetic field. By shaking them, you will get rid of these ions.

Now re-energise your hands before moving on to the treatment itself. This amounts to sending out through your hands the intention you have chosen for the treatment. Linger on those spots where you have noticed irregularities, putting the palms of both hands over them. Transmit energy through the right hand and receive it through the left. Release this vital force through your hands, programmed according to your intention and the colour you have chosen.

When you feel the exchange is complete, if necessary sew up the holes you noticed during your evaluation. To do this 'sewing', move your hands (one behind the other with the fingers spread out) over the hole, as though each finger was emitting a thread of light, and repair the patient's etheric tissue with these 'threads'.

Put your hands on the patient's feet, imagining roots of light from them burying themselves into the ground. If any surplus energy remains, it can now be eliminated by following these roots of light. Then put your hands above the person's head and call the celestial energy on to it so that it can receive the Creator's blessing for a return to good health. You can also spend a few moments praying for the patient.

The final stage involves discussing with the patient the effects felt throughout the treatment.

The therapeutic touch can be carried out in any position, whether lying or sitting down or standing up. But since the person being treated will very often experience some weakness, it is advisable to be seated. This also allows the patient to relax the whole body, which will enable you to move your hands round within the etheric field without any difficulty. This would not be so easy if the patient was lying down.

You must practise this therapeutic touch technique for several weeks or months before moving on to treatment with quartz crystals. This way, you can quietly acquire the necessary degree of mastery and some experience of the possible results. When you have established a minimum level of reliability, you can start work with the crystals without any fear of harming the patient. In fact, these two methods are similar. The only difference is that the crystal will strengthen the process set up by the therapeutic touch. It will also increase the effectiveness of your treatment around the patient and you will be surprised by the quality of the results you can achieve.

It is essential that you take time to perfect the therapeutic touch technique before moving on to treat patients with quartz crystals.

TREATING WITH QUARTZ CRYSTALS

༉

To start with, it is necessary to establish the right type of crystal with which to work. You must find a crystal that is neither too large nor too small. It must also be light enough so that you can manipulate it in your hand for periods of time that could exceed 30 minutes. It must not be so small that you have difficulty in identifying the C face of the crystal, the one which will enable you to change and orientate the energy. A crystal that is slightly smaller than your fist is the ideal size.

A clear quartz crystal has a point, leading to which there are six faces, the extension of its six sides. Each triangular face leading to the point is different. One of these faces is longer than the others and it is this one that we call the C face. If you move this face parallel to the palm of your hand, you will feel a kind of pencil of light scratching the surface of your hand. This is the ray of energy that the crystal sends out, because it is the C face which modulates its force.

To carry out treatment using a crystal, you must first of all focus yourself. Then imagine some roots of light coming out from your feet and anchoring you firmly to the ground. Following that, imagine a dome of clear light or even an amethyst light above you and the person you are getting ready to help.

Then energise your hands and evaluate the electro-magnetic field by holding both hands parallel to the patient's body on the surface of the etheric field, that is to say about 15 or 20 centimetres from the body. Question your patient to find out the spots where the problems exist and make the most complete evaluation possible in order to determine which colour is indicated for the treatment.

Now hold the crystal in front of the patient's spiritual plexus, that is to say at the point of the sternum between the solar plexus and the cardiac plexus. Press the C face against the patient and put your other hand on his back in order to feel the crystal's ray when it passes through the body. That will take between 30 seconds and a minute and a half. Its effect is to open the patient's energy field and chakras.

Next place the C face of the crystal on the top of the patient's head – on the fontanelle – and keep it there until you feel, with the hand holding the crystal, that this centre is open. Then gently lift the crystal towards the sky, as if you were pulling the patient's head upwards with an invisible wire. You will often have the impression that the head is rising, that the back is becoming straighter and that the head has greater equilibrium on the shoulders.

Following this, give the patient a 'crystal bath'. This involves passing the crystal all round the inside of the electromagnetic field, as if you were trying to stroke it, in a similar way to the sweeping principle used in the therapeutic touch. For this stage, you should hold the C face of the crystal parallel to the patient. The crystal will draw away the positive ions, thus freeing the electromagnetic field of those that have accumulated there. Equally, it will harmonise and balance the etheric field and even out those parts that are too deep or too shallow. It will also soften and smooth out those spots that were rough to the touch. This treatment will provide a general toning up of the field.

When you have finished, pass the crystal with your hand through some salted water for a minute or so, to clean away the positive ions it has accumulated from the electromagnetic field. Then wipe it well with a suitable cloth and focus yourself a second time.

At this point you can ask the person being treated to concentrate. However, it is important not to do so until this stage, because if you do ask him to concentrate before your evaluation, certain symptoms will disappear in the process. Therefore you must wait until you have finished your evaluation before letting the patient do this. When the patient concentrates at the same time as you, it is will be extremely beneficial for the rest of the treatment.

Once you have focused yourself, programme the crystal with your intention for the patient and infuse a particular colour, which you will already have chosen a little earlier. Obviously you can only programme a single colour into the crystal. Include, at the same time as the colour, your intentions for helping and healing and every suitable intention for encouraging a return to good health or an improvement in the well-being of the patient.

Having programmed the crystal, hold it about 30 centimetres above the patient's head, with the C face directed towards it, and help him to visualise the colour already programmed into the crystal. I will take an example of how to proceed using the colour blue.

Look at your patient and say to him: 'Imagine the colour blue spreading through your head, filling the whole of your brain, running through your hair, down your neck, on your chest, in your eyes, your nose, your mouth, your throat, flowing over your shoulders, down your clavicles, into your lungs and your sides and down your arms as far as the tips of your fingers. Imagine the colour blue running down into your diaphragm, your stomach and your abdomen, impregnating every one of your organs, and flowing past your hips into your legs, your knees, your calves, your ankles and into your feet, filling the whole of your body right to the tip of your toes with a refreshing and soothing blue light'.

Having guided the patient to visualise the colour permeating the whole of his body, take the crystal and work on the parts that need treating. Hold it 30 or 40 centimetres from his body, with the C face directed towards him, and move it clockwise, like the rotation of the sun in the sky, making a spiral of circles as you gradually work it closer to the body. As you approach with the crystal, reduce the size of the circles until, when you get very close, you sense a kind of little hook, as if the ray emitted by the crystal's C face was making a knot or being caught up. Now pull in this little 'hook' with your crystal, until you reach the outside of the field, and start again.

After you have done this several times, check the affected spot with your other hand. When you feel you have obtained the desired effect in the patient's field, tone up the area. To do this, move the crystal round in the etheric field, a bit like you did when you carried out the crystal bath, but limit yourself just to this spot. Then treat in the same way all the places which you felt contained problems when you made your original evaluation.

When you have finished, put your crystal in salted water to purify it of its programming. Now all that remains is to close up the patient's energy centres that were opened at the beginning of the crystal treatment. There are two ways of doing this.

The first consists of sweeping the field with an eagle's feather – or another type that is large enough to create a good air current – with a quick movement to cause a light wind. You must not use feathers from the vulture, crow or owl.

The other way of closing the energy centres consists of forming a triangle with your two hands, linking your thumbs and index fingers. Position this triangle in front of the patient's spiritual plexus and then move your hands up above the head and then back down in front of the body as far as the ground, all the time visualising that you are closing all the centres and thus resealing his energy body.

It is very important to close up these centres properly after treatment, because it can be dangerous for the patient if they leave with the centres still open.

After everything is over, you can ask your patient to give you their impressions and describe the sensations they experienced during the treatment. You can also ask them about their feelings since the treatment was completed.

On an energy level this treatment is very powerful. It is recommended that you repeat it several times, with a few days' interval between each, in order to really implant into the patient's energy body the vibrations required for his re-harmonisation and return to good health.

As with all energy treatments, the effect can wear off over a period of time. The treatment will continue to work particularly well in the first two days afterwards. Sometimes the patient can think his condition is worsening, that discomfort or pain have increased, or that other worrying changes have taken place. Such reactions are normal and you must explain clearly that when the body undergoes healing, it is sometimes possible to experience pain and changes that are not always pleasant. The process is not unusual and need not cause concern.

It is important to follow very conscientiously each of the stages that have been outlined. To forget or leave out any of them can sometimes compromise the well-being of the patient.

OTHER EXERCISES AND DISTANT HEALING

We are now going to look at a series of questions, called the 'eternal questions', which involve auto-evaluation. These questions serve to evaluate the changes that take place in a therapist's feelings while they perform the therapeutic touch. You can take these questions as a guide to help you understand the kind of changes you undergo when you are practising meditation and the exercises and healing techniques suggested in this book. In addition to this, I believe these questions can help you evaluate a variety of different experiences.

How do you sense your exterior environment?

On what occasions do changes occur in the way you perceive people and objects around you?

When do you feel that you are physiologically different? When do you sense changes in your heartbeat, your breathing, your muscular tone or the level of energy in your body?

How could you describe the way in which you feel your experiences?

To what degree can you grasp your inner conversation, when you are explaining to yourself what your senses are telling you?

On what occasions do you notice changes in your emotions?

According to your habits, do you think you over-react or under-react?

How do you use your memory?

Are you conscious of some continuity in what you experience?

When are you conscious of changes in your perception of time?

Does time go faster, slow down or stop?

What is your sense of identity, your perception of yourself?

What role have you the impression of playing?

When do changes occur in your mental, cognitive and evaluation processes?

Are there important changes in your logic or reasoning capacity?

How do you relate to your own physical image?

What feedback do you get from your movements, your postures or your body's energy 'waves'?

Do you react differently with the environment?

Do you feel involved in or detached from the people and objects living around you?

All these questions are quite subtle and the replies can vary according to the moment. You will not always reply in the same way; that depends on the circumstances and your stage of evolution. It is very useful to go through this questionnaire from time to time and compare your answers with previous ones. What you have replied and how this varies can help you to understand yourself better and give you a better understanding of what others can feel.

When you work with crystals, you can provoke in yourself and others states and sensations that are very different to those ordinarily felt. It is therefore important to tell the patient not to get alarmed and to reassure them that what is happening is normal. When people know that you have tried it yourself and are familiar with the possible reactions, they will feel much more confident.

There is a technique that enables you to communicate with a crystal in order to feel the personal experiences of the patient directly. Because you must never forget that a crystal is a living form. So how does it live? How does it feel? How does it hear? What is its life tissue? This is what you are going to experience by communicating with its way of existence.

To begin with, you have to understand properly what are called the 'body of light' and the 'body of darkness'. We have already talked about a body of light, which is the inherent perfection of every human being. At the start of our existence, our potential is limited and our being is as pure as its divine essence. Accidents of birth will produce inequalities, and disharmony and faults will be revealed which become what we call the body of darkness.

The body of light, however, is not dependent on the physical body. It is not restricted to it and has few limits in space or time. It can travel very quickly across time, space or different levels of the conscience. It is eternal.

For its part, the body of darkness is made up of our earthly experiences after birth. We must see its positive side and must love it as much as the body of light. It is our physical body, which allows us to experience what we have arrived on this earth to learn. It is also the reflection of our body of light. The body of darkness is the child who cries and has not been comforted, the child who has not been loved. It is all the faults that have been able to express themselves in the physical body since our childhood. This aspect of ourselves will reveal the disharmony and faults that are not a part and parcel of the body of light, but which well and truly make up a part of our present incarnation. It is our materialisation on the physical level.

The body of darkness is also what we call the 'ego' and, when experiencing communion with a crystal, it is important that you put this to one side for a few moments. To feel a crystal's life impressions properly, you have to commit yourself completely to the experience.

First sit down in the meditating position and focus yourself. Think about your body of light, resplendent in its beauty and perfection. Then think about the body of darkness that you are. Thus the body of light infiltrates the body of darkness, merges with it, fills it with its light and becomes as one with it. The body of light and the body of darkness now form a single being. The doors of hope open and the body of light projects itself into a large clearing in the depths of the forest and at the foot of a high mountain.

On this mountain, there are grottoes and caves and all sorts of stones, rocks and crystals. Inside the grottoes and caves and on the surface of this mountain you find all types of crystals and stones and you are drawn by one of these stones, one of these crystals. You hear the song of a crystal that sings for you. You feel yourself irresistibly attracted by this song towards one crystal in particular and you approach it. You allow yourself to be drawn by the piece of rock, this stone. You are standing in front of it and you look at it. Now your body of light penetrates inside the crystal and merges with it, becoming as one with the crystal.

And you yourself become this crystal or this stone. You

see, hear and feel what the crystal sees, hears and feels. Quite simply, you live in this life form, completely open and committed to the experience, you the crystal, you the stone . . .

After a little while, quietly leave the crystal and thank it for having shared with you its life, its being. Then return, passing back through the doors of hope and reintegrate your body. And very gently, when you feel ready, make a note of what you have been through.

This experience furnishes us with a lot of information that enables us to better understand our friends from the mineral kingdom.

When you have finished the search for your crystal friend, you can also follow a stream which runs into the ground in order to experience this stone in the depths of Mother Earth.

Here now is an exercise for purifying the chakras, the energy centres situated along the spine. Take a quartz crystal by its point, checking that it is not too large. (Because you will be putting it on your front, you can understand why it should not be too heavy.) Begin by focusing yourself, then look at the crystal and contemplate it for ten minutes. Then stretch out on your back and put the crystal on your front.

Imagine a clear, transparent light leaving the crystal and forming an arc above your body and penetrating the first chakra, at the base of the spine between the anus and the sexual organs. You are now in this light. Observe the first chakra; if there is any energy blockage, clear it with this light. Carry on by moving up to the second chakra and repeating the exercise; observe it and, if needs be, purify it with the help of the light. Continue purifying each chakra in turn until you arrive back on your front. Afterwards, do not forget to purify the crystal.

There is another exercise with the crystal that will help you find the answers to certain questions. Start by focusing yourself, then identify the question very clearly and consider all aspects of the problem, considering at the same time the answers that you have already obtained. Once you have really identified the question, hold the crystal in your right hand and lie down on your back and do what is called the 'free float'. Let the thoughts come to you without any interference. Let them flow freely without trying to influence them.

After a certain period of time, take some notes on all that has passed through your mind during this 'floating'. Then hold the crystal in your left hand, again lying on your back, and once again let the thoughts come to you without any restriction or influence. When you have finished, write down everything that went through your mind and then leave it all to settle for an hour, 12 hours, a day or even a week. The necessary period of delay will vary depending on the time you take to look at the material you have obtained with fresh eyes and an independent mind.

If you analyse what you have received from the left-hand part of the brain and then that from the right-hand part, what is revealed from this synthesis will provide the answer to your question. When you have the crystal in the right hand, it is the left-hand part of the brain which is influenced. Equally, when you have the crystal in the left hand, it is the right-hand part that is affected. The way you point the crystal has no effect whatsoever.

THE FOUR GRANDFATHERS

For all American Indians, the four cardinal points are among the greatest archetypes; they are the great angelic beings who watch over and look after the four corners of the universe and who are the source of inspiration and harmony on man's spiritual path. They are the four grandfathers who co-ordinate – with the spirits of the elements – the temperature and weather, be it sunshine or storms. Prayers for the American Indians always start with an offering to the four cardinal points, to the four directions.

At the centre of the medicine wheel that the four grandfathers form there is the human being. We all have a direction, which is our fundamental direction, but you must not develop just the qualities that belong to this direction. You should make a proper tour of the medicine wheel. You must strive to be perfectly balanced by having the qualities attached to each direction in order to blossom in a stable and harmonious way.

Let us take a brief look at the writings and symbolism associated with these four grandfathers.

Will and spirit corresponds with North. The American Indians talk of the world with the ideal form ('ungawi' or spiritual world) being to the North. If you want to speak with your ancestors or those who are not yet born, it is towards the North that you should turn. The animal associated with it is the great white bison.

The colour of North is white and its time is night and winter. In a person's life, it is the period when they have white hair, that is to say towards the end of their days when they meditate on what they have accomplished during their life. North's element is water. All hidden potential is found in the North and is symbolised by frozen lakes. Here is contained life's promise that has not yet been manifested; it is still frozen, waiting and invisible. As we continue to walk around the medicine wheel, the ice melts and the lake reveals the life it contains.

So, you reach East, which corresponds to the interior and exterior light, to illumination. We have a habit of saying that education comes from the East because it is the power of the imagination and the mind. The colour yellow and the golden eagle are associated with it. Knowledge, understanding, learning and inspiration are the qualities transmitted by the spirit of the East. It represents life's birth and is the dawn, the rising of the sun in the morning and the spring in the seasons' annual cycle.

South symbolises the power of growth, love, innocence and confidence. The two animals associated with it are the coyote and the little mouse. The former is the trickster, the joker, the one who plays games to make us learn and change despite our resistance. The latter represents innocence and candour.

The season of rapid growth which is linked with the South is obviously the summer. It is the childhood in one's life and the middle of the day. South's element is earth. It also symbolises the correct route towards our home, the red path, the right way which is a virtuous life full of respect for the works of the Creator. Its colour is red, although one also finds green here.

West is the direction of change, of medicine and of maturity. In the West are the dark waters of introspection where the beautiful shell woman (a representative of the Great Mother Goddess) lives in the Pacific Ocean. We talk of the Pacific Ocean as the mother waters and the Atlantic Ocean as the father waters. The way of medicine is to the West. This is the home of the black and brown bears, who teach the way of mysteries, methods of healing, herbs and healing rituals. The power of transformation and the thunder birds live in the West. These birds bring rain, thunder and lightning, which are the forces of transformation.

We associate the colour black with the West, as well as

violet because of its transforming power. West is the autumn, sunset and a person's maturity in life. Its element is fire. Death is the setting sun, through which the dead travel to rejoin the spirit world.

But the four grandfathers are certainly much more than all that. They are greater than one could possibly explain in mere words or speech. It is beneficial to feel the effect of each direction and you can achieve this through meditation or exercises that face each of the four directions in turn. The answer to any prayer addressed to the directions is always immediate. You can, with practice, sharpen your perception to feel it. Anyone who wants to live in perfect balance keeps right in the centre of these directions, absorbing the teachings that come from each of the grandfathers.

These forces are present in the traditions of the North American Indians and also exist in other traditions. They are great angelic beings, immense and very prolific in their manifestations and powers. It is to them that one customarily offers sage, cedarwood and scented hay at the start of prayers and meditation, presenting the shell containing the burning herbs to the North, East, South and West before offering it to the Earth and the Sky.

BLESSING A STONE

Here is a simple ceremony by which you can bless a stone or a crystal. First you must focus yourself and then energise your hands and make a triangle by linking your two thumbs and index fingers. Put your hands over the stone and move the triangle you have made with your hands towards the East. Bring the forces of the East on to the crystal. Next move your hands towards the South and bring them back over the stone, drawing into it the forces from the South. Repeat this same gesture for the West and then the North.

Now move your hands up in front of you the full length of your central channel (or spine), still keeping the triangle, right up to your head. When you have reached here, with the triangle still pointing upwards, move back down, with your two thumbs passing from the top of your head, in front of the third eye and down the length of the central channel. By now the point of the triangle must be directed towards the ground, just as you reach the top of your stone. The aim of these movements is to take the energy from your field and bring it on to the stone. Rest there until you feel a response coming from the stone, then make three clockwise turns with your hands before separating them quickly.

The first time you carry out this blessing, go through the following procedure:

Take two stones of the same size and, with your hands, evaluate the energy that these stones are giving out. Then take one of the stones, with which you will be carrying out the blessing ceremony as indicated above, and once again compare the energy that the two stones are producing. The one that you are about to bless will have a much stronger energy and its electromagnetic field will be much deeper. Your intention can certainly influence the nature of your blessing.

DISTANT HEALING

The first form of distant healing is prayer, which really is very powerful. I have seen people create tornadoes and then stop them with the power of prayer. I have also seen people do things which normally, according to the laws of physics, are impossible. Very often the power of prayer demonstrates the very reason for praying.

There are some healing groups who form a circle, hold hands and pray silently while one person in the centre carries out the therapeutic touch. This has an incredible effect, magnifying many times the power of this treatment. Some miraculous cures have been achieved this way, because the people who are working with you at that moment, to help and to cure, are charged with energy as if they were connected to a battery. They draw at the same time on this healing force of prayer and transmit it through whoever is carrying out the therapeutic touch to the person who needs to be treated. The type of prayer used is not important. What is important is the faith of the person praying.

The regular practice of prayer is an essential element in the training of crystal therapy. It purifies and nourishes the being. It also enables you to create a 'wire' or channel of energy along which frequencies favourable to healing can be carried. Distance is no obstacle and therefore does not exist.

A second stage involves the use of a clear quartz crystal,

which you place with its point towards you when you pray. Later you can also hold the crystal in your hands while praying. All your thoughts and words must be well controlled and directed because they will automatically be amplified by the crystal. Begin first by practising prayer and, once you have got into the habit, you can then use the crystal.

Another way of practising distant healing consists of using what I call a 'prayer board'. You must first find a 'witness' of the person to be cured. This could be a photograph, a lock of hair, a piece of writing by that person, a signature . . . in brief, something which comes from the patient or is directly connected with them. Place this witness in the centre of a square formed with boxes or wood and offer an introductory prayer or say to yourself: 'I call here now the powers and spirits of the four directions to come and help, cure and "shield this action"'. 'This action' is what you are doing and 'shield' signifies protection. After this short prayer, make a circle of sea salt around the witness.

Next programme your crystal (a pointed clear quartz) with your healing intentions and place it on top of the witness. If you are able to localise the person in the space, you should direct the point of the crystal towards him. Reprogramme the crystal seven times, that is once a day for seven days. It does not matter whether these days are consecutive or not, but they must come within a lunar cycle – that is to say within a period of 28 days. Repurify your crystal each time before reprogramming it. Wait 24 hours after the seventh reprogramming, then remove the crystal and the witness and dispose of the salt by burying it outside.

This is a simplification of a very ancient ritual taught by Oh Shinnah.

Another way of achieving a cure from a distance is the dream. Oneiri work is very important since it has a very physical effect, one that is very real in our lives and experience. The Indians have a habit of saying that one is in a dream, the Creator's dream. The Creator is in the process of dreaming the world and the universe and this is what we see around us.

They also think that life is a dream and that when we die, we wake into the reality of things, that is to say the spiritual world. There are plenty of planes and levels in the human consciousness. It is therefore important to control your dreams because they have a much greater impact than you would think on the fabric of your life.

The first stage consists of remembering your dreams and of waking up in the dream and being conscious of what you were in the middle of dreaming. Then it is a question of influencing the course of your dream. Once you have achieved this you will be able to heal in your dream.

To do this, before you go to bed in the evening, burn some cedarwood to purify the room you are in. Next, offer a prayer of gratitude for the day just passed. Once in bed, look back over the events of the day and make a mental note of them so that you do not forget to return in your dream to those things you did not fully understand at the time. When you have done something wrong (for example, if you have replied impatiently or aggressively to a request; if you have not been listening; if you have been brusque or indifferent . . .), put this right, change it by thinking about having had a more agreeable attitude at the time, a more open approach. Imagine the same events, but change the elements of your behaviour that were undesirable. This way you will accumulate less 'karma' and you will not have to come back to this event in your dreams.

Finally repeat the following nine times: 'I am going to remember my dreams'. And the next day, when you wake up, write them down.

When you have mastered this stage of memorising your dreams, before going to sleep repeat the following nine times: 'I will be conscious that I am the dreamer who dreams the dream during the dream'. The repetition of the same sentence nine times has a hypnotic effect, especially when you are on the point of falling asleep. This thought impresses itself very deeply on the subconscious.

During the dream, when you are conscious of being the one who is dreaming, take a look at your hands. (You can also, before sleeping, repeat nine times: 'I will see my hands in the dream'.) You can then lift your hands towards the sky in your dream and call on the forces there to bless the Earth, drawing your hands down towards the ground. When you have achieved that, you are ready for the next stage.

This amounts to travelling consciously in your dream. Choose an object or a place that has an important or symbolic significance for you. Before sleeping, repeat nine times: 'I am going in my dream towards my object (or place) of power'. When you have succeeded in doing this, you will be ready for distant healing through a dream. This stage consists of repeating nine times before going to sleep: 'With my body of light, I will go near (name of the person) to help and heal him'. The following morning – and particularly on the first occasions that you try this experiment – I suggest that you enquire about the health of that person. You will be surprised by the results.

The most useful stone for helping this dream work is the herkimer. I strongly advise you always to sleep with this stone when you are trying to heal through a dream. It helps awaken your consciousness in the dream, but in particular it protects you in your travels through the oneiric world. It is useful to programme this crystal with the appropriate intentions before you go to bed.

SUMMARY

O Shinnah of the Teneh tribe has given us some valuable insights into the American Indian Secrets of Crystal Healing.

All healing is spiritual and progressing your spirituality, cleansing and purifying your 'self', following a discipline of meditation will all heighten your natural healing powers. Slowly but surely is the key to all learning – true learning takes time.

Crystals come from the Mother Earth, so linking them with planetary energy and influences and gaining an understanding of this as outlined in Chapter Seven will give you a deeper understanding of the crystals. The healing energy of the crystals is very powerful. Taking care of your crystals, purifying them and treating them with respect will ensure that you will gain a valuable healing tool.

There are many different ways of working with the crystals – as outlined in Chapter Three – using tinctures, essences and the crystals. Working with your hands, understanding your own energy, using visualisation, the therapeutic touch and the powerful energies of colour in conjunction with your crystals will all help you to access the healing energies of the universe, connecting with and using the natural healing energies that are available to all of us.

Remember when healing the three fundamental laws: Unconditional Love, Non-attachment and Intention.

Ask yourself the 'eternal questions' in Chapter Eleven regularly and keep a diary of your answers – as you progress the answers will change and keeping a diary will allow you to see yourself evolve.

This book will guide you along your healing path and I wish you luck and much joy as you discover the beauty and power of the crystals as wonderful healing tools.

INDEX